W9-CBW-872

The Human
Resources
Revolution

Dennis J. Kravetz

The Human Resources Revolution

*Implementing Progressive
Management Practices
for Bottom-Line Success*

Jossey-Bass Publishers

San Francisco   •   London   •   1988

THE HUMAN RESOURCES REVOLUTION
Implementing Progressive Management Practices for Bottom-Line Success
by Dennis J. Kravetz

Copyright © 1988 by: Jossey-Bass Inc., Publishers
350 Sansome Street
San Francisco, California 94104
&
Jossey-Bass Limited
28 Banner Street
London EC1Y 8QE

Library of Congress Cataloging-in-Publication Data

Kravetz, Dennis J., date.

The human resources revolution.

(The Jossey-Bass management series)
Bibliography: p.
Includes index.
1. Manpower planning. I. Title. II. Series.
HF5549.5.M3K73 1988   658.3'01   87-46336
ISBN 1-55542-091-5

Manufactured in the United States of America

The paper in this book meets the guidelines for permanence and durability of the Committee on Production Guidelines for Book Longevity of the Council on Library Resources.

JACKET DESIGN BY WILLI BAUM

FIRST EDITION

Code 8819

The Jossey-Bass Management Series

Contents

Preface

Charles F. Kettering once said, "My interest is in the future because I am going to spend the rest of my life there." That is an attitude all of us should share, for the future is indeed where we are all headed. Those who anticipate it properly will benefit more than those who do not.

Concern about the future is particularly necessary when we think about the workplace, for there has been dramatic change during the past few years. Computers, robots, sophisticated telecommunications devices, new products and services, and many other changes have virtually reshaped the work environment of just a few years ago. Because the pace of change is accelerating all the time, many managers find it difficult to keep up with these new developments and manage them effectively.

While the change in workplace *technology* has been dramatic, it has been minor in comparison to the impact this change has had on *employees* in the workplace. For example, the use of a robot may improve the production process, but more important, it will drastically alter the work lives of many employees. Such technological changes will create new jobs that require new skills, knowledge, and training and eliminate the need for some existing jobs.

The Human Resources Revolution examines the revolution going on in the workplace, with a particular focus on its effect on employees. This book will provide detailed answers for managers struggling with the following questions:

> What sorts of employees will we need in the future?
> What kinds of skills and training will they need?
> Where will our new workplaces be based in the future?
> What sorts of management styles will be needed to supervise effectively in the new workplace?
> How should the new company culture and climate be established?
> What new jobs are emerging and how can we fill them?
> What organizational structure will be most appropriate in the future?

The workplace revolution we are experiencing today is more extensive than any change that has occurred in nearly 300 years. Managers need to be proactive and manage that change or it will manage them. For readers who want to create a workplace in tune with the future, I offer a simple challenge: let the ideas presented in this book stimulate you to come up with new ideas on your own. Then turn those ideas into concrete changes. By doing so, your company will attain greater financial success, as did many of the companies noted in this book.

I have based this book on my years of experience as a human resources executive, industrial psychologist, and consultant. I have always been fascinated by the human side of business—how productivity and financial success can be maximized through the effective management of human resources. Other reasons for writing the book include my intense curiosity about the future and my personal experience of having observed great upheavals in the workplace. The result is a practical book about the human resources side of the workplace revolution.

Many of the suggestions offered in this book are based on: (1) the actual programs of successful companies, (2) my own personal experience, and (3) the logical results of adjusting to the changes we are facing in the workplace. In addition, the suggestions I offer are based on hard data from the Survey of Organizations presented in this volume. The results of that survey show a very strong correlation between human resources progressiveness and financial success measured in sales, profits, and equity growth. The survey results offer powerful evidence that we are indeed witnessing a workplace revolution and that companies that take note and implement certain programs— such as participative management, work at home, and pay for performance—can be much more profitable than those that fail to do so.

Audience

The Human Resources Revolution will be of interest to managers and employees who are struggling to understand, prepare for, or introduce workplace change and who must effectively handle day-to-day activities at the same time. Human resources and line managers, in particular, will find this volume helpful because of its emphasis on human resources in the workplace. Detailed advice is offered on how to audit your company's current status and implement desired changes where they are needed. Case studies are used throughout the volume to highlight what leading companies are doing, and action steps are presented as a blueprint for getting the most out of human resources at your company.

Overview of the Contents

Chapter One describes the evolution of the workplace by examining the nature of jobs, workplace culture, leadership style, training, and many other human resources issues. I draw some startling parallels between the workplace of the past and the potential workplace of the future.

In Chapter Two, I discuss new technology, new industries, changes in jobs, and changes in the work force. The impact of these changes on people in the workplace is emphasized in particular.

Chapter Three presents the results of a major study of *Forbes* 500 companies. The results show that companies that are progressive in human resources management and in tune with the current workplace revolution have better financial results than those who are not. These conclusions are based on five-year trends in sales growth, profit growth, profit margins, equity growth, and company stock performance.

In Chapter Four, I present evidence that a new type of workplace is growing in importance—that workplace is the home. In this chapter, I cover methods of implementing work at home, as well as ways of addressing employee migration to the South and West United States, away from the major metropolitan areas.

The new type of organizational structure needed for the future is discussed in Chapter Five. I give specific advice on how to decentralize the workplace, flatten the management hierarchy, and structure compensation systems.

Chapter Six details the means to set up an ideal company culture and climate for the future. I point out the elements that will be necessary in such a culture and discuss communication and changes in company culture.

In Chapter Seven, I discuss the new types of jobs evolving in the workplace—jobs that offer the potential for more meaningful work, require a great deal of workplace freedom, and require generalized rather than specialized knowledge. I emphasize that without careful job design and an enlightened, participative management, the potential gains inherent with these jobs will not be realized.

In Chapter Eight, I present a detailed profile of changing employee demographics, including the aging of the work force, increasing diversity of the work force, increasing reliance on immigrants for staffing, and changes in the size of employee households and marital status. I include a detailed discussion of programs necessitated by these demographic changes, including employment contracting, flextime, flexible benefits, new criteria for hiring, and new hiring techniques.

Chapter Nine covers employee development, which has become very important due to rapidly changing technology and the needs of a better educated work force. I detail basic training and development, career development, and nontraditional training methods, such as productivity improvement and team building.

In Chapter Ten, I discuss new ways of managing that accommodate the recent workplace change. I illustrate this new management style—including the movement to general versus close supervision, participative management, the fostering of creativity in all employees, enhanced communications with a diverse work force, and new skills at staff selection and development—and explain how to implement it.

The Survey of Organizations is reproduced in the Appendix. With this, readers can assess human resources progressiveness at their own companies and compare their results to the *Forbes* 500 sample.

Acknowledgment

I would like to publicly thank the many vice-presidents of human resources and other executives who assisted me with the Survey of Organizations. They provided a great deal of detailed information about their companies that added immeasurably to this volume's comprehensiveness. Without their assistance, the conclusions presented in this book would be much less convincing than they are.

Rolling Meadows, Illinois   Dennis J. Kravetz
March 1988

The Author

Dennis J. Kravetz received his B.S. degree in psychology from Purdue University and his M.S. and Ph.D. degrees in industrial psychology from the University of Illinois, Champaign-Urbana. He is founder and president of Dennis J. Kravetz and Associates, a human resources consulting firm located in Rolling Meadows, Illinois. Formerly, he was vice-president of human resources at Heller Financial Inc. and director of human resources at Tandem Computers.

Kravetz is a member of the American Society for Personnel Administration (ASPA) and has served as the society's national vice-president and a member of the Board of Directors from 1982 to 1984. He has also served as chairman of ASPA's Personnel Research Committee and as a member of their Foundation Board from 1982 to 1984. As well, Kravetz is a member of the American Society for Training and Development, the American Psychological Association, and the Society for Industrial and Organizational Psychology. From 1982 to 1985, he served on the Advisory Board of Directors of Commerce Clearing House Publishers.

In 1979 and 1980, Kravetz received ASPA's Creative Application Award. This national award is given annually for the most outstanding creative application in the human resources field. Kravetz has published a number of articles on human resources topics and he is the author of *Getting Noticed: A Manager's Success Kit* (Wiley, 1985), which was also published as an audio-cassette series (Nightingale-Conant, 1987).

The Human
Resources
Revolution

1

The Evolution
of the Workplace

If you are a human resources or line manager, you have no doubt had to cope with a tremendous amount of change in the workplace in the past few years. That change is but a small part of a major technological revolution. Day-to-day management is so time-consuming and demanding that it is difficult to pull back and look at the big picture regarding this workplace revolution. This book will delve into the sources of the current workplace revolution and provide suggestions on how to manage it effectively.

The current workplace revolution is not the first that humanity has experienced. The agricultural and industrial revolutions had tremendous impact on the work environment. They not only changed the nature of the jobs and the workplace itself but affected culture, government, family life, recreation, and countless other aspects of our lives. While we recognize that technology affects our lives away from work, the focus of this book is on changes in the workplace itself—how the workplace revolution affects the nature of jobs, the physical workplace, management style, the types of employees who will be successful in such a workplace, and what the individual manager can do about it.

Before considering present and future workplace changes, we need to review the previous workplace revolutions. With the lessons we learn from them, we can incorporate the best aspects of our earlier work environments into our current and future workplaces and eliminate the shortcomings of the industrial revolution while going forward in an explosion of technology.

Hunter-Gatherers and Early Agriculture

Anthropologists tell us that our evolutionary history goes back at least three million years and that we attained our current form approximately 50,000 years ago. Despite that lengthy history, for all but the most recent 10,000 years, humans were nomadic hunter-gatherers. It is interesting to speculate how that long evolutionary history prepared us for the jobs of today, since our mental and physical characteristics have not changed since long before the start of the agricultural revolution.

Early humans were probably meat eaters, at first scavenging for meat and later hunting animals as prey. For some groups, this hunting evolved into the tracking of herds. In addition to meat, the diet included vegetables and berries, gathered wherever people happened to travel. Early ''work'' consisted of providing food, shelter, clothing, and tools for the family group.

Life remained this way for nearly three million years, with little change aside from the domestication of some animals and a slight improvement in tools. Dramatic changes began about 15,000 years ago, when the glaciers began to retreat and the earth's climate became warmer and wetter. That new climate, while beneficial for agriculture, was less advantageous for the large grazing animals, which began to die out.

By 5,000 years ago, agriculture was a fixture in most of the world, and it remained that way until the beginning of the industrial revolution, around 1700. From being nomadic hunter-gatherers, people became sedentary farmers, harvesting crops, domesticating animals, and making many more personal possessions, since a sedentary life-style allows for more possessions than does a nomadic one.

Assume that you were able to transport yourself back to the time of hunter-gatherers or ancient farmers. You might ask questions such as the following: What would the workplace be like during this time? What kinds of jobs would people be doing?

How fulfilling would these jobs be? What sort of leadership style would be most effective? What type of training and skills were required to be proficient at work?

Although early humans did not "hold jobs" in the sense that we use that term today, certain tasks were necessary for survival, and it is useful to compare how these were done with our current work practices. Our lengthy evolutionary history may have prepared us for a certain type of work, a certain type of leadership style, and a certain type of work environment, and our current workplaces may not take advantage of what we do best.

Fortunately, there is some fairly good evidence as to what the early work environment was like, though it may be necessary to speculate at points. To get a clear understanding of the workplace of the past, the following twelve areas will be examined in detail:

- Job content
- Job meaningfulness
- Workplace freedom
- Individual need fulfillment
- Workplace culture
- Career choice
- Place of work
- Leadership style
- Available technology
- Centralization of work
- Training and skills requirements
- Migration patterns

Generalist Jobs. The "jobs" of early humans were of a generalist nature. To ensure the family's continued existence, all of the skills of survival had to be known and practiced by everyone. The untimely death of a specialist could have cost the lives of the entire family group. So, rather than jobs being specialized, everyone had a role in providing and preparing food, tending fires, moving possessions, and making clothing and implements. There was a simple division of labor based on gender, with men concentrating on hunting and tool making and women concentrating on collecting plants and berries and rearing children.

Jobs continued to be generalist oriented after the agricultural revolution. Much of the work focused on food production. Land had to be plowed, seeds planted, crops tended to and harvested, various foods made from grain, and domesticated animals taken care of. In addition to agriculture itself, part of the typical "job" involved building a home and furniture and making clothing, tools, and many other personal possessions. There was probably still a simple division of labor between men and women, with men handling the more physically demanding work.

Job content was richer in the agricultural period than in hunter-gatherer times. The making of numerous personal possessions and controlling the food-production process provided a wider variety of tasks to be performed. These richer jobs more fully challenged people's skills and abilities. But people remained generalists to ensure that they could start new farms of their own or continue running those of their families. A specialist who knew only some of the tasks would not be able to do this.

Highly Meaningful Jobs. Jobs vary in their meaningfulness—the degree to which individuals see a link between the tasks they perform and some meaningful whole. Did hunter-gatherers see their work as meaningful—did they see their tasks as contributing to the overall group's success? Their work must have been highly meaningful. If a game animal was killed, the participants could easily see how this work led to a larger goal, providing food for the family unit. The same would be true for gathering fruit and berries, cooking, and making tools and clothing. Individuals doing this work would clearly see it as meaningful and contributing to the survival of the family group.

Jobs continued to be highly meaningful during the agricultural period. Activities such as planting seeds, cultivating crops, and tending animals would easily be linked to a larger goal, providing food and surviving. Building a home, making furniture, and making clothing and personal possessions would clearly be linked to the larger goal of providing shelter and comfort. There was a direct and clear link between job tasks and larger group goals—if you worked hard and skillfully, you would fulfill your basic needs and survive.

High Workplace Freedom. Managers today are familiar with the concept of "workplace freedom"—the amount of discretion in decision making, opportunity to control the pace of work, variety of job tasks, and opportunity to be creative and learn on the job. Our ancestral hunter-gatherers had much workplace freedom in carrying out their jobs. There was a high amount of individual freedom to decide when and where to hunt, forage, sleep, make tools, and relax. The only restrictions on individual decision making involved when the group would move on and when to jointly hunt for large game, and it is believed that decisions in these areas were made cooperatively. The job pace was affected only by the need for additional food or shelter; otherwise, people hunted or foraged at the pace they preferred.

There was a great deal of task variety in these early jobs, though the tasks were repetitive. Opportunities for creativity and learning were abundant. The nomadic movement from place to place required adaptation to diverse new conditions that were completely uncharted and unknown. Changes in climate, terrain, plants, and animals all required learning and a flexible, open perspective.

Workplace freedom remained high after the agricultural revolution. Workers did not have "bosses" (except for their parents), so deciding where to plow, what to grow, when to slaughter, and when to start or quit work was left to the individual. Similarly, there was no machine or supervisor controlling the job pace. That was the choice of the individual, dictated only by the needs of the crops, the food supply, and the desire for possessions. An individual's work pace might determine how prosperous that person might be, but it was the individual's choice to make.

Creativity, learning, and ingenuity were highly utilized during the agricultural period, as witness the large number of inventions and discoveries during this time. These included the wheel, new metals, the plow, many tools, irrigation, pottery, new crops, and a very large number of personal possessions. In sum, freedom in the workplace was very great in the lengthy period before the industrial revolution.

Moderate Need Fulfillment. Abraham Maslow (1954) has ranked basic human needs as follows: (1) physiological—food, water, and rest; (2) safety—protection against danger, threat, and deprivation; (3) social—belonging, association, friendship, and love; (4) ego—self-esteem, competence, status, and recognition; (5) self-fulfillment—realizing one's full potential.

Early humans were no doubt most concerned about fulfilling physiological and safety needs. Obtaining food, water, shelter, and protection probably required most of their time. Fulfillment of social needs was mixed, being strong within the work group and limited on the outside because of the absence of links to other groups and constant mobility. Ego and self-fulfillment needs were probably not fulfilled at all.

Workers in the agricultural period were probably better able to fulfill their individual needs than their hunter-gatherer predecessors had been. Agriculture permitted more storing of food, making it easier to fulfill physiological needs. Homes, shelters, and better weapons provided for better fulfillment of safety needs. Social need fulfillment also increased as a result of the increased contact provided by villages, towns, and tribes, though many people still lived in remote areas. Ego needs were partially fulfilled, since making one's own home, possessions, and food contributed to strong self-esteem. Needs for status and recognition and for self-fulfillment were unlikely to be met.

Strong Workplace Culture. Workplace culture can be thought of as the degree to which people feel they belong to and identify with others at the same workplace—the degree to which there is a common set of goals, purpose, values, and philosophy among co-workers. Workplace culture can vary greatly from group to group. Was there a workplace culture long ago? Was it a strong one?

Evidence suggests that early humans had a very strong sense of workplace culture. The members of a typical work group of about thirty people hunted together, foraged together, ate together, lived together, and even played together. There was frequent contact within the work group and a common sense of purpose and need for mutual support in order to survive. Because of the vast distances between groups and the difficulty in communicating, this culture is not likely to have extended beyond the group itself.

Workers during the agricultural period were also likely to experience a strong workplace culture in their extended family groups of twelve or so members, who produced food together, made possessions together, and also lived, ate, and played together. That made for a strong bonding and a sense of common purpose and mutual support. As with the hunter-gatherers, workplace culture was not likely to exist outside of the immediate work group because of communications difficulties and the lack of a common "organization" to bind together the individual farming groups.

Another aspect of workplace culture is the degree to which the workplace is governed by policies, procedures, or guidelines. Hunter-gatherers and those of the agricultural period were remarkably free of policies and procedures. In fact, these terms are not even meaningful within this context. There was no right way to do early jobs, and hours were set by individuals. Although there were *suggested* ways to obtain food, hunt, or make possessions that no doubt passed from generation to generation, this carrying out of tradition was a far cry from prescribed rules and regulations.

Limited Career Choice. Was there much in the way of career choice for people in the hunter-gatherer or agricultural periods? Could individuals select what they wanted to be? The opportunity for career choice was very limited prior to the industrial revolution because of the focus on obtaining food and shelter. There was a simple division of labor along gender lines but no real ability to choose a certain type of career. Everyone was a generalist to ensure that food-production skills and tool-making ability did not die out. There was no option to work part time or not to work at all, as some people have now.

Home as the Workplace. Today, most of us think of the workplace as an office building or factory, but that was not the case in our earlier history. For hunter-gatherers and farmers, the workplace and the home were one and the same. There might be occasional forays away from the home base to obtain food, but these would not likely take people very far away. It is only in relatively recent times that people have been journeying away from home to go to work. During the agricultural period, the workplace (farm) became stationary instead of moving from place to place, as it did with hunter-gatherers. The workplace came to have a defined location and size, since the farm had discrete geographical boundaries. These changes foreshadowed events to take place in the industrial revolution.

Participative Leadership Style. What type of leadership style did early "supervisors" have? Was it autocratic? Participative? Anthropologists believe that hunter-gatherer groups were led by a few dominant males, who assumed their positions by virtue of being the best hunters in the group; in other words, experience and skill led to leadership. The work group had relatively few decisions to make, aside from when to hunt or move on. Given the relatively small number of decisions needed, there was little need for a controlling autocrat. In today's jargon, the leadership style was participative, with most decisions made through a collaborative process. There was only one level of supervision, and that was very general supervision. People probably followed the leaders willingly, without coercion.

During the agricultural period, the leaders were the parents of the farm family. Their style was also probably participative, with children and other family members being given general direction and instruction, then left to carry out their tasks. The leaders (parents) had work to do as well, and this, if nothing else, would prevent close supervision. Of course, in some respects, the parental role can be thought of as autocratic, and no doubt the employees (children) sometimes experienced it in this way. But by and large the day-to-day performance of job tasks was supervised in a more participative than autocratic style. As with the hunter-gatherers, there was only one level of supervision.

Technology Based on Food Production. Early technology was highly focused around food production. The tools were primarily for killing prey or preparing food for eating. The technology of this time was very slow to evolve, and it was not until about 10,000 B.C. that the spear, bow and arrow, and food containers were common.

The technology of the agricultural period was also based on food production, though there was an explosion of inventions during this time. Work-related innovations included the plow, sickle, wheel, harness, and cart and the use of animals as the first "machines" to do farm work. Communications improved during this period with the invention of printing, which allowed people more easily to share knowledge about work.

Decentralized Work Environment. Hunter-gatherers worked in a decentralized environment for millions of years. Both the work group and the living group consisted of small numbers of individuals, and there is no evidence of links between work groups during this time. The evidence further suggests that there was no centralized structure within the group itself; individuals and bands operated autonomously.

Workers of the agricultural period also operated in a decentralized work environment. The work group was small and, in most cases, not linked with other work groups. Even where a kingdom or empire linked people within a region, individual families still carried out their work in a decentralized environment.

Long Training, Many Skills. Managers of today, whose mentally demanding jobs require a number of diverse skills and fairly lengthy training, may tend to minimize the mental skills required for jobs of earlier times. However, it must be remembered that we had to develop our mental potential from somewhere, and that somewhere was our past. Certainly, hunter-gatherers had to have physical abilities to hunt various prey, but many mental skills were required as well. For example, archeologists have found evidence of ancient pits where animals were lured and killed. The construction and camouflaging of such pits took skill in planning, organizing, and anticipating the future—higher-order mental skills much more advanced than mere physical abilities. Animals were often tracked as well, which required analytical skills in determining the type of animal, its direction, and how long ago it had passed the area.

Early people's movement from place to place required learning and adaptation to new and different climates and foods. Anticipating seasonal changes, determining migration patterns, and recognizing poisonous foods could well make the difference between life and death. The learning of these various skills would no doubt take a lengthy period of time.

Mental skills were necessary during the agricultural period as well. Certainly, the planting, cultivating, and harvesting of crops were physically demanding, but the mental skills were probably more important than the physical. Figuring out which seeds to plant, where to plant, how to cultivate and irrigate the land, and nurture the crops required planning, organizing, foresight, and patience, as did domesticating and raising livestock. The building of homes, furniture, and countless personal possessions required creativity, learning, and flexibility, since there was no blueprint to follow and no easy way to learn the skills. As with the hunter-gatherers, a lengthy apprenticeship program would be necessary for a person to become highly skilled at the job.

From Nomadic Wanderer to Sedentary Farmer. The last work environment factor to be considered is that of migration. Where was the source of work? Did it change over time? For early humans, migration was slow but constant. People moved to be nearer the source of food, to follow animal migration patterns, or simply to see whether conditions were better elsewhere. Thus, the work site was constantly changing throughout our early history and followed no particular pattern. Remains of people of more than 10,000 years ago have been found in virtually all parts of the earth.

Migration changed dramatically during the agricultural period. At the beginning of this period, people moved inland as rising water levels from melting glaciers engulfed the coastal plains. When agriculture took hold, those who lived in woody or hilly areas migrated to fertile plains. After this initial migration to fertile lands, people tended to remain sedentary, since that was a necessity for agriculture. The work site, and home site, took on a more permanent nature.

The Industrial Revolution

Though the agricultural revolution represented a dramatically different way of life from the hunter-gatherer life-style, workplace characteristics remained relatively unchanged. The jobs were new and different, but they presented many of the same challenges and opportunities as previously. That was to change completely with the industrial revolution, which represented not only a new life-style but a radically different workplace as well.

While the majority of the population still lived in rural areas prior to 1700, the village grew in importance after that. Craftspeople began to concentrate in the villages, and a significant cottage industry developed. Rural farmers brought more and more work to these cottage industries and bought more goods in the villages.

The world's population increased dramatically during the agricultural period, from perhaps 10 million in 8000 B.C. to 625 million by A.D. 1700. That large sedentary population demanded more and more in the way of products for work and enjoyment. Overseas trade in Europe also increased dramatically in the years before 1700. World trade demanded more in the way of products for exchange with other nations and to supply growing colonies abroad. This set the stage for industrialization.

No one knows exactly what started the industrial revolution, and no doubt there were several factors involved. But perhaps the strongest factor was the need for more finished products for a growing domestic population (eventually over three billion) and for overseas commerce. The local, village-based cottage industry would find it hard to keep pace with these demands, since individual craftspeople were not geared to quick mass production but instead focused on the slow, individual tailoring of products. The harnessing of machines for mass production was the ideal solution to the problem.

Early mass-produced goods included farm implements, textiles, watches, and firearms. Later came railroads, steel, automobiles, aluminum, chemicals, appliances, and countless other goods. The mass production of such goods was cost-effective and therefore enjoyed great success. Those who could build larger and faster machines no doubt had the edge over their competitors.

Blue-collar manufacturing jobs were the typical jobs of the industrial period. Their numbers as a percentage of all jobs continued to grow during this period, largely at the expense of jobs in agriculture, reaching a peak in 1940 and declining ever since. By 1960, the "end" of the industrial period, a new technology had unfolded, and white-collar jobs had come to dominate. Blue-collar workers currently make up less than 30 percent of the U.S. work force, with white-collar and service workers constituting more than 60 percent.

While blue-collar manufacturing jobs predominated during the industrial period, there were many clerical and office positions as well that were similar to the blue-collar jobs—not in actual job responsibilities but in opportunities for growth, creativity, place of work, and training and skill requirements. We discuss these and other workplace factors of the industrial period (1700 to 1960) in the remainder of this section.

From Broad Generalist to Narrow Specialist. A typical job of the industrial period, such as assembly-line worker, was routine, repetitive, and specialized. In contrast with the earlier periods, when a single individual would make an entire product from beginning to end, an employee of this period would typically perform just one task in making the overall product, with other employees or machines performing other specialized tasks. The same task, such as making welds on an automobile frame, would be repeated over and over again. There was little opportunity for learning and adapting, a big difference from the past. Machines made the overall manufacturing process more complex, but they made the average job more simple.

Less Meaningful Jobs. Job meaningfulness, the degree to which job tasks are seen as being related to some meaningful whole, suffered a great deal during the industrial period. No longer could employees produce an entire product for personal consumption, as people did during the hunter-gatherer and agricultural days. Instead, they worked on bits and pieces of the entire production process. In many cases, the employee never saw the entire assembled product but knew only his or her small role in the process. Each individual's effort and output were harder to link to the goals of the entire work group. Someone making welds on an automobile frame had a difficult time linking that task with a production goal for finished automobiles.

Another factor that affected job meaningfulness during the industrial period was the receipt of money for work performed. Prior to the industrial revolution, individuals produced goods for their personal consumption or to barter for other goods. It was easy to see a link between the work and the reward, which was usually food. But now people received pay instead. This might seem like a trivial difference, but it had a great effect. Because the job tasks themselves lacked meaningfulness, it was all the more important for the output to be seen as meaningful. But now employees had a more difficult time seeing how their day-to-day tasks were related to some final goal. They knew only that once a week they received a paycheck for the time spent working. A symbolic element was placed between work and the obtaining of food or other products, decreasing job meaningfulness.

A Loss of Workplace Freedom. Freedom in the workplace practically disappeared during the industrial period. Gone were the opportunities for creativity, learning, and ingenuity. The job tasks simply did not require employees to learn, adapt, or innovate. Only a very limited number of specialists, such as engineers and managers, had the opportunity to be creative in designing machines and work procedures.

The average employee contributed little to development, functioning instead to merely carry out the repetitive tasks not done by machine. During the agricultural period, innovations in the workplace-home were developed by the average employee. Now, however, employees had to find away-from-work outlets for creativity.

Early humans and agricultural-period humans had ample opportunities to make decisions in carrying out their jobs. But that changed with industrial jobs. An employee whose job was inserting metal plates into a stamping machine might have occasion to make decisions only if the machine broke down or the employee ran out of plates. And even these problems were solved not by the employee but by an expert, be it the repair person or the boss. Decision making, an important component of earlier jobs, was virtually eliminated during the industrial period.

Freedom in the workplace was also lessened in terms of job pace. As Bronowski (1973) said, the domination of men by machines was "a new evil that made the factory ghastly" (p. 280). Employees no longer had the opportunity to work at their own pace. Now they had to move in synchronization with machines, with the ever-present pressure to move faster and faster.

Only Basic Needs Fulfilled. Industrial-period jobs fulfilled only lower-order needs. Physiological needs such as food, water, and rest were fulfilled during the industrial period as in preceding times. Safety-need fulfillment, next on the hierarchy, probably deteriorated during the industrial period, since jobs were now much more dangerous than agricultural jobs. Powerful machines posed a new threat of physical injury that did not exist in pre-machine agriculture. Safety and hygiene conditions in early factories were also very poor, presenting new health hazards.

Social needs could be better fulfilled in the industrial period than in earlier times. Bringing together large numbers of workers in a common workplace permitted the development of more social contacts than were possible in a rural workplace. Working in a company also created a feeling of belonging and association, a new experience for people at this time.

Ego needs, only partially fulfilled during the agricultural period, were probably even less fulfilled in the industrial period. To support one's family no doubt contributed to ego fulfillment in both time periods. However, while agricultural-period employees had meaningful work, industrial employees worked at tasks that were not challenging, so that ego-need fulfillment was lessened. Nor was the need for status and recognition fulfilled during the industrial period.

As during the agricultural period, self-fulfillment needs were not met by industrial jobs. No employee could feel self-actualized and working at full potential in basic assembly-line and manufacturing occupations. These jobs were far from being stimulating and challenging and offered little in the way of growth and personal development.

Weak Culture, Strong Regulation. The industrial revolution decreased culture within the immediate work group but increased culture across work groups. It would be very difficult for the average employee in a factory to feel as close to co-workers as had his or her counterpart in the agricultural period. No doubt close friendships formed in factory settings, and there was opportunity to meet many people. But most of those associations would not be very strong, certainly not as strong as those among people living and working together every day, as occurred in farming. The sheer size of factories also made it difficult to know a large number of people closely and created feelings of alienation.

Where workplace culture did improve during the industrial period was across work groups. A large company with multiple manufacturing facilities enabled employees to identify with a larger unit, the company itself. Employees might not personally know those at the other facilities, but they would know that they all worked for the same organization and were thus linked together. Unions would likewise produce a feeling of common culture that was missing in farming environments. On the negative side, unions produced many culture clashes with management, which made relations worse.

There were tremendous changes in the workplace during the industrial period with regard to policies and procedures. Hundreds of rules and regulations were developed during this period, unlike earlier times. Since workers on assembly lines had to be there at the same time, there was a need for common work hours, common lunch hours, and common break periods. The opportunity to pick one's own hours did not exist.

The industrial period saw the development of a ''right

way" to perform a job, as advocated by people such as Frederick Winslow Taylor and his "scientific management." Each job was broken down into components, and each step was standardized as to how it was to be done, with what tools, and how long it would take. Work rules proliferated in many other areas as well. There were policies on what type of clothing to wear and how to be groomed. There were standardized pay scales, standardized benefits, standardized grievance procedures, and standardized requirements for entry into jobs. There were procedures on how to apply for a job, procedures for taking a leave, procedures for calling off sick, and procedures for taking a vacation. Company personnel policy manuals often covered just about any area imaginable. All of these policies and rules represented a radically different work environment from that of our ancestors. While the policies helped control a large business, one could question whether they represented any progress.

More Job Choices. The industrial period saw the development of many highly specialized jobs, giving employees the freedom to pursue any of a number of different careers. This was one of the few benefits resulting from the industrial revolution. This freedom of choice should not, however, be overstated. Many of the jobs that employees could select from were repetitive tasks in assembly or manufacturing that did not require much in the way of skills. Henry Ford once said that there were 7,882 specialized jobs in the automobile assembly process alone. While there was freedom to select, the actual variety was fairly limited.

From the Home to the Factory. During the industrial period, the home and place of work came to have separate identities, the first time in history that this was the case. Employees now traveled to their place of work, typically a manufacturing facility in a city. Though we now take this for granted, the change had dramatic effects on the lives of many people. The most obvious was that families were now separated for much of the day while working spouses labored at their jobs. This eliminated the parental role in providing job training to children.

Other changes involved working for an entity called the

"company" and producing goods not for personal consumption but for use by others. The terms *company, employer,* and *employee* began to have meaning only during the industrial period. People who had learned to be self-sufficient and fend for themselves were now dependent upon the company for their jobs and livelihood. The company became a sort of parent, taking care of the employee's basic needs but keeping the employee in a state of dependency as well.

The industrial period saw the development not only of larger and larger factories but of larger and larger offices to support those factories as well. Toffler (1980) correctly points out that the industrial revolution was almost a contest for bigness— with companies and countries trying to outdo each other for the biggest facilities. That bigness created a sense of being "just another number," a cog in the wheel that had little impact on the company's overall success.

The Rise of the Autocrat. The industrial revolution produced the first true bosses in workplace history. In the past, the leaders had been senior family members, who are believed to have used a participative management style. Was leadership during the industrial period participative as well? Not in the least. The type of management advocated by Taylor and others was that of very close supervision. It was believed that employees were lazy and would not do a good job on their own but had to be closely watched and motivated by someone else. As Taylor said, "The work of every workman is fully planned out by the management at least one day in advance, and each man receives in most cases complete written instructions, describing in detail the task which he is to accomplish, as well as the means to be used in doing the work" (Heisler and Houch, 1977, p. 66).

Taylor and others like him also believed that the typical employee was incapable of contributing new ideas to the job and making decisions. Taylor wrote, "Any improvement which the workman makes upon the orders given to him is fatal to success" (Rogers, 1974, p. 53). He advocated a very strong, decisive, controlling type of management. And while a departure from any style seen before in our long evolutionary history, it is exactly this controlling, authoritarian management style that has predominated right up until the present time.

The industrial period saw the development of a steep, many-leveled management hierarchy, unlike the single supervisory level of prior workplaces. Now, the man at the top was very often never seen or known by the employees at the bottom. That produced an alienation of sorts, creating a psychological distance between employees and those who ran the company.

Technology Based on Machines. Technology expanded at a great rate during the industrial period. Certainly *the* invention of the period was the machine. Machines enabled the manufacture of countless products that could not be made by hand. Mass production by machine tremendously increased production capability over that of earlier cottage-shop methods. Significant advances were made in transportation, with the development of the train, commercial ship, automobile, truck, airplane, and jet. Other new technology for the workplace included new materials (steel, plastics, vulcanized rubber, and aluminum), new energy sources (gas and electricity), and a large number of scientific measuring devices. Advances in architecture and construction enabled the building of large factories and office buildings.

Despite all of these advances in technology, the typical employee's job did not change throughout the industrial period. Employees were largely adjuncts to machines, and routine jobs such as feeding products into a machine or filing order forms were not changed by the introduction of more sophisticated machines. The elimination of certain manufacturing jobs by technology did not occur on a large scale until the 1960s, when the industrial period was at an end.

A Centralized Work Environment. The industrial revolution led to much centralization. The typical company structure centered around a large corporate headquarters in a major city. Reporting to the corporate headquarters might be geographical divisions, product groups, or subsidiaries of the parent organization. To these units in turn, individual manufacturing plants or other facilities would report. In industries such as steel and automobiles, many of the facilities were concentrated in one geographical area to make control easier.

It was rare for individual manufacturing facilities to operate in a decentralized way. Reporting relationships were made clear, and only a few individuals in the corporate headquarters could make major decisions affecting operations. The production facilities were merely there to carry out the operating decisions from above; they were but a small piece in the overall centralized operation. This centralization was very different from life as a hunter-gatherer or farmer, where there was no link between work groups and there was freedom to operate without control from above.

Short Training, Few Skills. The skills required for the typical industrial job were less diverse than those for an agricultural-period job. Performing simple assembly work or feeding products into machines did not compare with "big-picture" jobs such as raising farm products and livestock and making all of one's own personal possessions. One could thrive in an industrial environment with a narrow range of skills, and those with very diverse skills and talents would find the routine aspects of the work dull and monotonous.

Industrial jobs did require physical skills, especially eye-hand coordination. What was missing from industrial jobs was the ability to think, innovate, and change work procedures, skills that had previously determined individual success or failure. Also missing was the ability to plan and organize for the future, as was done in raising produce and livestock. Industrial jobs required that an employee merely implement what someone else had decided to do or what the pace of the machines dictated.

The jobs of the industrial age were very easy to learn. Training would typically take no more than a day or two. Mastery from that point on was merely seeing how fast or how accurately the work could be done. There was no opportunity to learn from the job; it was mere repetition. Perhaps the greatest consequence of the industrial period was that it left people ill prepared for other types of careers, since employees had no broad-based skills. Their only realistic option was to find other, similar work.

Movement into the Cities. Migration during the industrial period had a very clear direction—into the cities. Urban areas with populations of 2,500 or more contained only 5 percent of the U.S. population in 1790. By 1850, this figure had climbed to 15 percent; by 1920, it was 51 percent; and by 1960, the end of the industrial period, over 70 percent of the population lived in urban areas. Every one of the largest U.S. cities had grown during the industrial period, though some had started to show declines at the end of that period. The same is true for large cities in other parts of the world as well.

The reason for the growth of the cities is obvious; that was where the jobs were. Companies building large factories needed to locate them where major transportation networks were available and large work forces could be recruited. That started a vicious cycle—once some factories moved to a larger city, more people moved there, bringing still more industry, and so on.

The major urban growth in the United States took place in the Northeast and Midwest. These areas were quick to develop an industrial base, while the South remained more agricultural and the West was late in being developed. The Northeast and Midwest also had better navigation routes and railroads for the shipment of products. But while the early "tilt" of the country was toward the Northeast and upper Midwest, this would radically change by the end of the industrial period.

The migration to the cities also changed the nature of the family unit. In the agricultural period, families were typically large, and extended families that included grandparents or uncles and aunts were common. Large families were necessary for the harvesting of crops and all of the other tasks that had to be done. But the industrial period was characterized by the nuclear family of two spouses and their smaller number of children. That was all that was needed to do the "job" of maintaining the household; extra relatives would be difficult for a single wage earner to support.

The workplace of the industrial period was a step backward in comparison to earlier workplaces. While technology and production advanced, the work environment deteriorated for the typical employee. Machines created unpleasant, boring work that offered little in the way of learning and creativity. Table 1 summarizes the changes that occurred in the workplace through this period.

Table 1. The Workplace Through the Industrial Period.

	Hunter-Gatherer and Agricultural	Industrial
Job content	generalist	specialist
Job meaningfulness	high	low
Workplace freedom	great	narrow
Need fulfillment	moderate	very basic
Workplace culture	strong	moderate
Career choice	limited	some choice
Place of work	home	factory/office
Leadership style	participative	authoritarian
Technology	food production	machines
Centralization	decentralized	centralized
Training, skills	long, many	short, few
Migration pattern	from nomadic to farmlands	from farmlands to cities

2

The New Workplace: From Smokestack to High-Tech

The typical workplace has clearly changed a great deal since the industrial period, and today's managers must manage this change. It is change of a much grander scale than a few new pieces of equipment and some new employees. It is a revolution of the same magnitude as the industrial and agricultural revolutions. Others have called this new revolution in the workplace the "second industrial revolution," the "computer revolution," or the "postindustrial period." Regardless of the name, something very new and different has replaced the old workplace. To manage the process effectively, a manager needs to understand the roots of the change, what is fueling it, and what can be done to run a profitable, successful business from here on out. This chapter considers the causes of the current workplace revolution—changes in the nature of jobs, new technology and new industry, and changes in the work force—and then explores some of the implications of these changes.

From Smokestack to High-Tech

There has recently been a rapid decline in the number of jobs in traditional industrial organizations in the United States, including steel, metal production, machinery, mining, railroads, rubber, textiles, shoes, and shipbuilding. Even the auto industry has seen some great declines, though a modest recovery in jobs has since taken place. In 1970, according to the American Iron and Steel Institute, the steel industry employed 512,000 people (Kearns, 1984). That figure has now declined to fewer than 236,000 jobs, nearly a 54 percent reduction. These figures are not atypical for traditional smokestack America. A report entitled *The U.S. Industrial Outlook* (1985) revealed some of the biggest job losers. In a period of just three years, the following numbers of jobs were lost in certain industries:

Steel	276,000
Heavy construction	123,000
Railroads	122,000
Construction and oil machinery	120,000
Fabricated metal production	59,000
Metalworking machinery	57,000
General industrial machinery	46,000
Farm machinery	43,000
Coal and lignite mining	42,000
Specialized machinery	33,000
Motors and generators	26,000
Fabricated metal products	25,000
Shipbuilding and repair	24,000

Clearly, the types of jobs being lost are blue-collar jobs, those that make up traditional industrial organizations. The percentage of blue-collar workers in the work force has been declining for forty years; they now make up less than 30 percent of the total. And what is replacing these jobs? The biggest gainers during this same three-year time period, with the numbers of new jobs for each, are the following:

Eating and drinking places	445,000
Personnel agencies	216,000
Grocery stores	165,000
Computers and data processing	136,000
Hospitals	127,000
Electronic components	126,000

Nursing and personal care	124,000
Physicians' offices	120,000
Legal services	110,000
Dentists' offices	72,000
Brokerages	70,000
Communications equipment	53,000
Accounting and auditing	51,000

The gainers were jobs involving services or high-tech products such as computers. Of the twenty industries that *lost* the most jobs, sixteen produce goods and only four supply services. Of the twenty industries that *gained* the most jobs, seventeen supply services and only three produce goods. The trend in the 1980s has been for four new service or high-tech jobs to be created for every production job lost.

Currently, managers and professionals outnumber unskilled laborers by five to one in the United States. Public school teachers alone outnumber all of the production workers in the chemical, oil, rubber, plastic, paper, and steel industries combined. Clearly, there has been a major shift in the types of jobs being created and eliminated, signaling the end of the industrial period. And this trend will continue in the future. Most traditional manufacturers have probably seen this type of job change in the past few years. They may call it "temporary layoffs," "reductions in staff," "downsizing," or "restructuring," but all these terms reflect the same outcome. Many of the traditional blue-collar jobs have disappeared permanently.

Some might argue that the loss of blue-collar manufacturing jobs in our more traditional industries is simply due to foreign competition. For example, twenty years ago, only a small percentage of all steel bought in the United States was imported from abroad. Recently, the figure is more like 30 percent. Steel industry personnel contend that if the imports were cut back substantially, employment levels would climb upward from their depressed levels and the industry would return to its former prominence.

But the issue is much larger than foreign imports. Many Third World countries are just now entering the industrial period in full force, while the United States has already left it. The Third World, by virtue of cheap labor and investing in new plants, can compete effectively for traditional manufactured products. We have "exported" our industrial-period jobs to these other countries. Even if this were not the case, the changing nature of American technology, economy, and industry would still bring about a decline in traditional manufacturing jobs. The service and high-tech areas are where the growth is occurring. The stimulus to add more jobs here would diminish the importance of traditional manufacturing even if these industries were not going overseas. We have become a service-oriented economy.

Industrial employment will not disappear completely in the United States. The trend will resemble that in agriculture, which once provided the vast majority of jobs in this country and now provides approximately 3 percent of the total. Traditional industries and blue-collar manufacturing jobs in this country are already becoming less and less of a factor in our economy. Such jobs will decline to perhaps 5 percent of the total in the next century. A "new wave," as Toffler (1980) puts it, will have replaced the old.

What does a human resources or line manager do about this change in jobs? Very specific advice on how to audit your practices and manage these new types of jobs will be offered in later chapters. For now, it is helpful to recognize that this type of change is broad in scale, and other companies are going through it as well. One thing you could do is examine your company and explore the opportunities for growth in the service or high-tech area. Is there a service end to your manufacturing business (for example, a consumer credit business that finances the purchase of your manufactured products) that can be added or expanded? Can an acquisition be made in the service or high-tech area? Should you diversify into other areas rather than remain a manufacturer of traditional products? Are you (and the union, where applicable) working toward retraining employees with limited job skills to prepare them for more service-oriented jobs?

New Technology and New Industry

The current revolution in the workplace is being fired by dramatic changes in technology. Foremost among these changes has been the development of the computer. The use of computers in the workplace has grown tremendously in the past twenty years. All major businesses have been affected one way or another by computers, and so have many of our jobs, not to mention our personal lives.

Many manufacturing procedures formerly done by people are now done by computer-controlled equipment. On the white-collar side, computers have eliminated much of the manual, routine drudgery that was present in accounting, finance, personnel, scientific, and research work. Clerical and secretarial jobs have been affected as well. No longer do secretaries spend significant amounts of time typing, correcting, and filing text. It is now done more quickly and easily with a word-processing software package. In some cases, secretaries may not do this work at all, since their bosses may have word-processing computers and do the work themselves. The paperless office is becoming a reality in many places, and, with it, the disappearance of file clerks and typists is also being seen.

Another significant technology change of the past few years has been in communications devices. The chief executive officers (CEOs) of organizations can now talk and be seen instantly by all of the employees in the company by means of satellite or cable transmission. There are teleconferencing centers where one can have a "meeting" with people across the country without leaving the office, being seen and heard and even sending data to the parties at the other end instantaneously. That is a tremendous change in our ability to communicate with others.

Facsimile machines enable the transmission of reports, memos, and data by phone line instead of conventional mail. And electronic mail has even replaced facsimile devices, enabling written material to be instantly transmitted around the world by satellite and computer. We are also very near the point where employees can speak directly to computers to dictate memos or issue instructions. These voice-activated computers have already been used on a limited basis with handicapped people. Commercial versions are starting to hit the marketplace now.

Robots are another tremendously important technology

change that is affecting the workplace. The use of robots has grown rapidly in the manufacturing sector, particularly in the automobile industry. Firms such as General Motors have made a significant investment in robotics, recognizing that the field will continue to grow. Robots have taken over many of the dangerous or more repetitive tasks of manufacturing, such as welding. This trend will continue, and probably explode, when robots have the ability to "see"—to distinguish objects on the basis of touch—and make decisions on the basis of the information gathered. Some robots already have limited abilities to do this.

The AFL-CIO Committee on the Evolution of Work (1983) has estimated that by 1990 there might be as many as 100,000 robots and 20 million computers in use in the workplace. The World Future Society (1984) forecast a 30 percent annual increase in the number of robots in the United States, versus a 2 percent annual increase in the human population. Clearly, these technology advances are the wave of the future. They will find their way into more and more arenas as time goes along.

Entirely new industries are evolving and affecting the workplace and type of employees needed. Some of these new industries are centered on the new technology just discussed. Such new industries include computers, semiconductors, communications equipment, robots, space exploration, and genetic engineering. And what types of jobs will these industries create? To be certain, there will be some manufacturing positions, such as computer cabinet assemblers. But many of the jobs in these new industries are white-collar or service, such as computer designers, service technicians, trainers, and software programmers. The fact that these *industries* are rapidly growing means that the number of white-collar and service *jobs* will grow as well, irrespective of the decline of traditional manufacturing companies.

Other industries on the rapid rise include accounting, consulting, health care, personnel agencies, and law firms. These firms are, by their very nature, white-collar and service oriented. The core jobs in these industries are professional positions requiring college degrees. And even the staff support employees in these industries are more highly skilled than the traditional file clerk or typist, for the more complex technology in the workplace requires a higher skill level than before.

What can a manager do about this industry trend toward service and high technology? First of all, recognize that these new industries require different kinds of people and different kinds of skills from those needed by the industries of the past. Is your company in tune with these new requirements? Are you hiring and training to increase "people skills" and technical skills such as computer usage? Very specific suggestions on how to do this are offered in Chapters Eight and Nine.

Changes in the Work Force

Another key factor spurring a revolution in the workplace is the composition of the work force itself. Today's work force is substantially different from that of the industrial period. One of the key differences is the amount of education attained. In 1940, the median number of years of education attained was 8.6, according to the U.S. Department of Commerce (1975). By 1980, this figure had increased to 12.7 years, an increase of 48 percent in just four decades.

In 1900, the heart of the industrial period, 29,400 bachelor's degrees were being granted annually in the United States. By 1980, over 1,000,000 bachelor's degrees were being given annually, according to the U.S. Department of Commerce (1975). In 1900, only 1,600 master's degrees and 382 Ph.D. degrees were given out in the United States. By 1980, 208,000 master's and 30,000 Ph.D. degrees were being awarded annually. In the ten years from 1970 to 1980, the percentage of the population with at least some college education increased from 21.2 percent to 31.1 percent.

This more highly educated work force has a different set of expectations from those of their less-educated counterparts. In particular, they want more meaningful work, work that allows creativity, thinking, learning, and the development of new skills. Employees with this higher level of education have come to demand this sort of opportunity in the workplace. Not to receive it would mean that the extra education and ability to learn would go to waste, leading to frustration and dissatisfaction, as is well known by any manager with a clerical employee who has a master's degree.

This more highly educated work force of today also wants a "career," not a "job." That is not to say that money or security is unimportant to today's employee, but the employee today works for much more than the pay, benefits, and security. Boring, repetitive work that might have been tolerated by the employee's parents or grandparents is not being tolerated by today's employee. There is no question that employee career development is one of the "hot buttons" in today's organizations. The establishment of career planning, succession planning, and employee development programs has been a high priority for many companies, which recognize that without such programs in place, they will suffer the consequences in employee frustration and low morale.

Part of this desire for a "career" is a result of the tremendous amount of information about careers to which people are being exposed. There are now entire sections of bookstores devoted to career planning, job search, career development, and the like. Schools are offering more career guidance than in the past. The net result is that employees today have high expectations for career development when they enter the workplace.

In addition, the traditional "vertical ladder" career path is disdained by many employees. They are no longer content to go from Accountant I to Accountant II to Accountant III. Instead, employees are more interested in cross-training, job rotation, lateral moves, and special projects that ultimately lead to their long-term career goal. And if the company has no system to address this need, dissatisfaction results.

A major survey of a large number of companies by the Public Agenda Foundation (Yankelovich and Immewahr, 1983) found that employees today are demanding higher levels of discretion in their jobs—more freedom to work independently in carrying out their assignments and the ability to set their own pace and make their own decisions. A 1982 study by the Work in America Institute (Rosow and Zager, 1982) found that "Ten years ago, 70% of industrial workers were willing to accept managerial authority with minor reservations. Today the reverse finding has emerged: younger, more educated workers resent authoritarianism'' (p. 23).

And what about the work ethic in today's employees? Has it deteriorated? The Public Agenda Foundation's study (Yankelovich and Immewahr, 1983) found that nearly two-thirds (62 percent) of the employees surveyed said they would prefer ''a boss who is demanding in the name of high quality work'' (p. 4) and that they want to do the very best they can. The study concluded that ''the conventional wisdom of a deteriorating work ethic is badly off-target; the American work ethic is strong and healthy, and may even be growing stronger'' (p. 4). The problem that was identified was the ''striking failure of managers to support and reinforce the work ethic'' (p. 5). The typical management style of today is still oriented toward the industrial period instead of the current workplace.

What can be done about the new type of employee in the workplace of today? First, jobs must not be designed with the boring, repetitive, task-oriented characteristics of the past. To tap the higher education and desires of today's work force, a higher level of discretion must be designed into nearly every job. More challenging projects permitting growth, learning, and development need to be the norm for even staff support jobs. Not to build this into jobs produces frustration and wastes much of the employee's capabilities. Second, career development and guidance programs need to be in place within each company. The focus must be on careers and not on jobs. Third, management style cannot continue to be autocratic and controlling. A participative, delegating style is much more compatible with today's work force and today's jobs.

A Revolution in Human Resources

I have chosen the year 1960 to mark the beginning of the current workplace revolution. That is when the workplace began to be dominated by the new technology, new industries, new jobs, and new work force, with the industrial period clearly on the wane. The current revolution is in its early stages, and we are still making the transition into this new work environment.

Much of what has been written about earlier workplace revolutions placed a heavy emphasis on the new products and new technology—the things—that these revolutions brought about. The agricultural revolution resulted in new food products—plants, grains, and domesticated livestock. The industrial revolution is known for mass-production techniques and the use of machines. Certainly, the *things* that came from these earlier revolutions had a major impact on the lives of nearly all.

Other writings have emphasized the social and life-style consequences of these earlier revolutions. For example, the agricultural revolution brought about a sedentary life-style and led to an increase in personal possessions. The industrial revolution led to bigness in factories and cities and the resultant problems of crowding and crime.

Interestingly, relatively little has been written about the workplace prior to the industrial revolution. Yet that workplace is worthy of note because of the dramatic upheaval that occurred with the industrial revolution. The workplace changed 180 degrees, moving from the farm to the factory, from participative leadership to autocratic leadership, from great freedom in the workplace to virtually none, from generalist jobs to specialist jobs. The effects of this revolution on *people* and on the *workplace* were much more dramatic than the technological and social aspects. The machines were not an end result but actually a *cause* of a revolution affecting people in the workplace.

It is easy for a human resources or line manager to get caught up in the technology side of the current workplace revolution. One can marvel over the new computing power of the latest portable computer, be dazzled by how quick and easy it is to use electronic mail, or figure how the latest robot will improve your department's productivity. But just as with prior workplace revolutions, we need to think about the impact of this technology on people and the workplace itself so that we do not make the mistakes of the industrial revolution.

The title of this book, *The Human Resources Revolution,* stresses the importance of people, human resources, in the current workplace revolution. To be successful, managers need to focus on the "people side" of the equation rather than the "thing side." The importance of people in the success of a company will continue to increase with the movement toward a service-sector economy. People will become the only product—a product that must be managed effectively during rapidly changing times. So it really is a *human resources* revolution and not a computer or technology revolution. Consider for a moment just a sampling of the human resources issues related to the new workplace revolution:

1. The typical jobs of the human resources period will involve different responsibilities from those required by jobs of earlier workplaces. How should these jobs be designed? What kinds of activities and responsibilities should people have?

2. A higher skill level is required by the new jobs. It takes more knowledge and skills to service and maintain a robot or operate a computer than to do assembly-line work or routine clerical jobs. What kinds of skills do employees need? What is the best way to identify and select these employees? What kinds of training and education will the work force require?

3. The workplace will need a different organizational structure, and perhaps a different physical location. What type of structure will be ideal from a human standpoint? Where will jobs be based in the future? What kinds of employees will be best suited to the new workplace?

4. Employees of the human resources period will have different expectations, needs, and demographic characteristics from those of their predecessors. What type of company culture will work best with this new work force? How do you establish such a culture? What sort of reward programs will work best? Will the workplace need many policies and rules or very few?

5. New types of employees, different jobs, a new culture, new technology, and a new company structure and workplace present a great deal of challenge for any manager. Will our former, more autocratic management style make it in the future? Is a new management style needed? What are the key characteristics of this new style?

These are all tough issues to be dealt with in the future, and they are all *people-related* issues. The list presented here is but the tip of the iceberg in comparison to all of the issues that will come up during the human resources revolution. Thoughtful planning and a number of skills will be needed by managers to successfully deal with these human resources areas. How to do this will be covered in depth in the remaining chapters of this book.

Coming Full Circle

The industrial period was, in many ways, a step backward for employees in the workplace. What does the human resources period promise to offer? Will it be another step backward, or a step forward? The human resources period has the potential to produce the most fulfilling workplace yet. But that word *potential* cannot be emphasized enough, for it is only by doing the right things that this potential will be realized. Otherwise, we will advance technologically but still be standing still with regard to the human resources issues.

Table 2 presents what the human resources period has to offer. It is interesting to note that the future bears similarities to the past. Our new workplace takes the best from the earlier work environments while adding new potential all of its own. This change represents coming full circle. The industrial period may have been nothing more than a 300-year anomaly in our history. Our early work history prepared us for the workplace period we are now entering, not the one we are just leaving.

Not everyone will step eagerly into this workplace of the future; there will be some resistance to such a transition. A painful example of this occurred in the Chicago area, which was particularly hard hit by the downturn in the steel industry. A group of former USX employees went to court numerous times to prevent their former employer from demolishing an antiquated steel plant, which had not employed anyone for several years. The group hoped that their actions would bring back the plant and their jobs.

The current workplace revolution cannot be stopped by court actions any more than farmers could have stopped the industrial revolution by protesting. The jobs and manufacturing plants that are disappearing will not likely ever return again. The actions of any one company or industry are small in com-

Table 2. The Workplace—Past and Future.

	Hunter-Gatherer and Agricultural	Industrial	Human Resources
Job content	generalist	specialist	generalist
Job meaningfulness	high	low	high
Workplace freedom	great	narrow	great
Need fulfillment	moderate	very basic	many needs
Workplace culture	strong	moderate	strong
Career choice	limited	some choice	great
Place of work	home	factory/office	home
Leadership style	participative	authoritarian	participative
Technology	food production	machines	computers
Centralization	decentralized	centralized	decentralized
Training, skills	long, many	short, few	long, many
Migration pattern	from nomadic to farmlands	from farmlands to cities	anywhere

parison to this larger trend in the workplace. The real issue is how to manage this change effectively; how to be proactive and anticipate where we are going and train and develop our employees for the new workplace.

Some companies may have anticipated this change in advance of its actual occurrence, or been quick to react to it. This means that they are now in sync with the workplace of the human resources period and will remain so in the future. Is there a payoff for doing this? Does it affect the financial success of a company? The next chapter details the results of a major survey of the largest U.S. corporations that was undertaken to answer these questions. The remaining chapters offer recommendations for action based on these results.

3

Human Resources
Progressiveness
and the Bottom Line:
A Survey of Organizations

Companies in tune with the current workplace revolution have made many changes over the past few years. Their efforts have gone well beyond bringing new technology into the workplace. They have instituted new programs, services, and operating philosophies that emphasize the human side of the workplace. Others have been slow to react to the new workplace. Perhaps they purchased some new equipment to upgrade their facilities but did little else to operate in concert with the current and future trends.

Does this difference in responsiveness to the new workplace affect bottom-line results? For example, are companies with progressive management styles, career development programs, significant training efforts, and a people-oriented culture more profitable than companies that are less progressive? It would seem likely that those that change with the times are more profitable than those that fail to adapt, yet there is no concrete evidence to back this up.

The degree to which companies have adapted to the new workplace is called ''human resources progressiveness'' in this book. As mentioned earlier, the revolution in the workplace *is* a human resources revolution, so *that* part of the name seems fitting. The term *progressiveness* refers to operating in concert with the current and future workplace, rather than experimenting with radical programs or spending exorbitant amounts of money on human resources programs. A company high in human resources progressiveness understands the critical importance of people to the bottom line and operates with this in mind.

The author conducted a major study to test the idea that human resources progressiveness is related to company financial results. It was hypothesized that companies high in human resources progressiveness have enjoyed more sales growth and profitability than those that are less progressive. Such progressiveness might even carry over to company results in equity growth and stock performance. While the current revolution in the workplace is quite young, results over the past five years or so should indicate whether any such trends have developed. Over longer periods of time, the trends might be even more dramatic.

For this study, company human resources progressiveness was measured through a specifically designed questionnaire and follow-up interviews, and data on several critical measures of financial success were collected on each company to see whether progressiveness is related to financial success. Details on the survey process and actual results follow.

The Questionnaire

The questionnaire used for the Survey of Organizations and a description of how it was developed are presented in the Appendix. The questionnaire contained fifty-one questions pertaining to human resources progressiveness in the following areas:

- Communications progressiveness
- Degree of emphasis on people in the company culture
- Degree to which management is participative
- Emphasis on creativity and excellence in the workplace
- Extensiveness of career development and training
- Effectiveness in maximizing employee job satisfaction
- Degree of recognition and reward for good performance
- Usage of flextime, work at home, and part-time employment
- Degree of decentralization and flattened management hierarchy

Each question was answered on a five-point scale, with higher scores indicating greater human resources progressiveness. A total score for human resources progressiveness was obtained by summing the scores across all items. It was this total score that was used to determine whether progressiveness was related to company financial results.

Measures of Financial Success

Financial information was collected on each company that participated in the Survey of Organizations. This information was drawn from *Business Week's* annual special issue (''1984 Scoreboard Special Issue,'' 1984) on company results, which presented data originally prepared by Standard & Poor's Compustat Services, Inc. The measures examined were those that were believed to best indicate the degree of success the companies had experienced through the year 1984, including the following:

- Five-year growth in sales
- Five-year growth in profits
- Five-year growth in dividends
- Five-year growth in earnings per share
- Five-year growth in common equity
- Price-earnings ratio for the latest twelve months
- Profit margin for the latest twelve months

Statistical significance tests were used to determine whether there were differences in financial success between companies that were high in human resources progressiveness and those that were less progressive. All results reported were statistically significant unless otherwise noted. Further details on the statistical significance tests can be found in the Appendix.

Companies Selected

A total of 500 companies, all among the largest 1,000 companies in the United States, were chosen to participate in the survey. Most of these companies appeared in the *Forbes* 500 list ("The 500 Annual Directory," 1984). Many of the companies were manufacturing organizations, though the sample also included service organizations, transportation companies, banks, and nonbank financial services organizations. Altogether, some thirty-six different industry groups were surveyed. Copies of the questionnaire and general instructions for completing it were sent to each company. Most questionnaires were completed by vice-presidents of human resources. Follow-up interviews were conducted in a number of the companies to validate the information and obtain additional details of company practices.

General Results

A total of 150 companies were retained for the final study (several were eliminated because of mergers, acquisitions, or incomplete questionnaires). The average human resources progressiveness score for all companies was 154.4, with a range of 83 to 211 (the maximum possible score was 254). The 20 highest-scoring companies and their scores are listed in Table 3. IBM led all companies, followed by Tandem Computers, Tektronix, and American Medical International. The highest-scoring companies covered a broad range of businesses and industries, suggesting that human resources progressiveness is not restricted to certain industry groups.

Companies were classified into industry groups according to their Standard Industrial Classification numbers. Table 4 presents the companies that scored highest in human resources progressiveness for each of sixteen major industry groupings. The highest-scoring industry group leaders were from the fields of computers, scientific equipment, and service companies. The lowest-scoring were from textiles, metal manufacturing, and machinery. All industry groups showed variation in scores, with some companies scoring considerably higher than others. Individual company characteristics would appear to account more for human resources progressiveness that does type of industry.

Table 3. Highest-Scoring Companies in
Human Resources Progressiveness.

Company	Human Resources Progressiveness Score
IBM	211
Tandem Computers	207
Tektronix	204
American Medical International	195
Rockwell International	194
General Mills	193
Merck	192
Perkin-Elmer	191
Hospital Corporation of America	189
3M	188
McCormick & Company	188
Boeing	182
General Foods	181
American Hospital Supply	180
Hewlett-Packard	179
Marsh & McLennan	178
RCA	178
Dun & Bradstreet	177
Libbey-Owens-Ford	177
Kimberly-Clark	176

Impact on Company Financial Results

Companies were grouped into three categories according to their human resources progressiveness scores. The top third, whose with scores of at least 166, were called "highly progressive"; the middle third, with scores between 148 and 165, "moderately progressive"; and the lowest third, "less progressive." The scores of the highly progressive companies were contrasted with those of less progressive companies to measure the impact of human resources progressiveness on company financial results. These two groups were clearly high or low in human resources progressiveness, making it easier to evaluate this impact. Moderately progressive companies, on the other hand, may be in a state of transition or not equally progressive on all indicators, making it difficult to evaluate the impact on company financial results.

Table 4. Industry Group Leaders
in Human Resources Progressiveness.

Industry Group	Company	Human Resources Progressiveness Score
Mining, oil, and refining	Ashland Oil	173
Food and related products	General Mills	193
Textiles and apparel	HARTMARX	164
Furniture, paper, and wood	Kimberly-Clark	176
Chemicals, pharmaceuticals, and allied products	Merck	192
Metal manufacturing and metal products	Commercial Metals	165
Computers and office equipment	IBM	211
Electrical/electronic products	RCA	178
Ships, railroads, and other transportation	Boeing	182
Measuring, scientific, and photographic equipment	Tektronix	204
Wholesale and retail trade	Southland	173
Finance and insurance	Marsh & McLennan	178
Service companies	American Medical International	195
Conglomerates	Rockwell International	194
Miscellaneous manufacturing	3M	188
Machinery (excluding electrical)	Rexnard	168

Table 5 presents the most critical findings of the entire study, the relationship of human resources progressiveness to financial results (means and standard deviations for the entire sample can be found in the Appendix). First, it may be seen that the highly progressive companies had an average score of 178.9 on human resources progressiveness, whereas the less progressive companies averaged 127.8. This difference is highly significant in both a statistical and a practical sense.

Certainly one of the most critical indicators of company success is sales growth rate. The highly progressive companies had annualized sales growth of 17.5 percent per year over a five-year period, while the less progressive companies averaged only

Table 5. Human Resources Progressiveness and Financial Results.

	Highly Progressive Companies	Less Progressive Companies
Average human resources progressiveness score	178.9	127.8
Annualized sales growth, five-year trend	17.5%	10.7%
Annualized profit growth, five-year trend	10.8%	2.6%
Latest annual profit margin	5.3%	3.3%
Percentage of companies having loss in last year	0%	18.0%
Annualized equity growth, five-year trend	16.7%	9.3%
Annualized growth in earnings per share, five-year trend	6.2%	– 3.9%
Latest price-earnings ratio	15.1	13.8
Annualized dividend growth, five-year trend	13.4%	9.2%

10.7 percent. This means that the highly progressive companies had 64 percent greater sales growth each year than the less progressive companies, and this was the trend for five years of sales results. The correlation between human resources progressiveness and sales growth was .29. Clearly, there is a very strong relationship between human resources progressiveness and sales growth.

Another way to understand the difference in results between the highly progressive and less progressive companies is to examine what would happen if the less progressive firms could attain the sales growth of the highly progressive. If the 500 companies included in our survey grew at only the rate of the less progressive (10.7 percent per year), sales growth for the entire group would increase by $298 billion in the next year. However, if sales grew at the rate of the highly progressive (17.5 percent), sales growth in the next year would be $488 billion. The difference between these two growth figures is a phenomenal $190 billion a year.

Next examined was the annualized company growth in profits, measured again over a five-year period. The highly progressive companies had an annual profit growth of 10.8 percent, while the less progressive companies had but 2.6 percent annual growth. This a difference of *315 percent* between the two groups. Highly progressive companies are increasing profits *each year* more than four times as fast as the less progressive companies. That is a tremendous finding, indicating a very strong relationship between human resources progressiveness and company profit growth. The correlation between human resources progressiveness and profit growth was .24.

Profit margins for the most recent year were also examined. Highly progressive companies had margins averaging 5.3 percent, while the less progressive companies averaged 3.3 percent, indicating that the highly progressive companies had profit margins 61 percent greater than their less progressive counterparts. The correlation between progressiveness and profit margins was .37. If companies low in human resources progressiveness could increase profit margins to the levels of the highly progressive, an extra $56 billion dollars would be added to the profits of the 500 companies included in our survey each year. That is a tremendous potential, and the evidence strongly suggests that human resources progressiveness is the way to achieve it.

Another startling result pertained to whether a company had shown a profit or loss in the most recent fiscal year. A total of 18 percent of the less progressive companies had shown a loss in the most recent year, whereas *none* of the highly progressive companies had shown a loss. Once again, the evidence indicates that human resources progressiveness is related to profitability.

Examined next was the annual growth in company equity, measured over five years. Table 5 shows that highly progressive companies averaged a 16.7 percent growth in equity each year. The less progressive companies had an average annual growth of 9.3 percent. This means that the highly progressive companies were increasing their equity base nearly 80 percent faster than their less progressive counterparts. The correlation between progressiveness and equity growth was .31. Once again, this is impressive evidence of a link between human resources progressiveness and financial results.

Impact on Company Stock

Does human resources progressiveness relate at all to a company's stock results? Table 5 indicates that the highly progressive companies showed an average annual increase of 6.2 percent in earnings per share. Companies that were less progressive showed an average annual *loss* of 3.9 percent in earnings per share. The correlation between progressiveness and earnings per share was .37. The evidence was quite convincing that there is a close link between earnings per share and human resources progressiveness.

Another variable looked at was the company price-earnings ratio. This variable showed the least difference between the two groups. The highly progressive group had an average price-earnings ratio of 15.1, while the less progressive companies had a ratio of 13.8. These results, while in the same direction as the other results, were not statistically significant (the correlation was .05).

A close examination of the results showed that in the less progressive group, one company had a price-earnings ratio of 99, another 90, and another 43, while none of the other less progressive companies had a price-earnings ratio greater than 30. The average ratio for the less progressive group was heavily influenced by these three companies, which may account for the lack of significant group differences.

The last variable studied was the annual dividend growth rate, measured over the most recent five years. Highly progressive companies had a dividend growth rate of 13.4 percent, whereas the less progressive companies had a growth rate of 9.2 percent. The higher figure was 46 percent greater than the smaller. The correlation of progressiveness with dividend growth rate was .18 (this was significant at the .10 level). The results here indicated a moderate relation between human resources progressiveness and dividend growth rate. The far-reaching effects of progressiveness on attaining better financial results appeared to carry over to stock performance as well.

Conclusions from Findings

The results of the Survey of Organizations were very compelling. Nearly every financial criterion examined showed a strong relation to human resources progressiveness. The more progressive companies had much better financial results than the less progressive firms. The results were significant not only from a statistical standpoint but from a practical standpoint as well. The magnitude of group differences in sales growth, profit margins, and other criteria has a tremendous impact on each company's success. If the less progressive firms could attain the financial results of the highly progressive companies, not only would individual companies be better off, but the national economy would improve greatly as well.

Some might argue that the results do not prove that human resources progressiveness causes better financial results but show only that the two are related. They might suggest that having a highly successful company causes a firm to be more progressive in its attitudes toward employees rather than the other way around. In other words, instead of causing good financial results, human resources progressiveness might be the *result* of financial success. If so, the same results presented in this book would have been obtained.

While this causation is possible, it does not seem as likely as the other way around. It is difficult to envision why, solely because of its financial success, a company would change its management style, have more employees work out of their homes, or change the company culture to one strongly oriented toward people. Many companies, if they are enjoying great financial success, are not likely to change, figuring that "you shouldn't fix things that don't need fixing." They retain their same successful practices until these need to be abandoned to address a static or declining market position. Success is not likely to breed this type of change.

Others might argue that success will give a company the financial wherewithal to do things they could not do before. But only a few items on the survey (training and communications programs, for example) entail increased costs. Most of the items (for example, management style, company culture) do not involve increased costs, and a few (such as work at home) actually represent a *savings* for the employer. The net conclusion is that financial resources do not drive the tendency to be progressive in human resources.

There is one last, compelling way to refute the idea that financial success causes human resources progressiveness rather than vice versa, and that is the companies themselves. Were their reasons for becoming progressive because they had large profits or because they wanted to operate with employees in mind to *maximize profits?*

The history of IBM and people such as Thomas Watson, its founder, has been well documented in a number of sources. IBM operates the way it does regarding people not because of early financial success but because it believes that this is the best way to manage people and run an organization. During the course of the Survey of Organizations, many examples were cited by those in the company to back up this idea.

Further, consider Tandem Computers, the company that had the second-highest score in our Survey of Organizations. Tandem is a youthful company, founded by Jim Treybig in the mid 1970s. When Treybig was starting up Tandem, and long before the company had built or sold a computer, he put together a master game plan for the company's future. That game plan included not only what would be unique about the company's products but what its philosophy about people and the company culture would be. Many of the items in the survey labelled ''progressive'' were incorporated in that early plan of Treybig's. So it was not company financial success that caused human resources progressiveness at Tandem, but the other way around. Tandem, by the way, has had tremendous financial success, progressing from a start-up company to one with over $500 million in sales in less than ten years, and doing this without merger or acquisition but only through internal growth.

The situation is similar at many of the other companies in the highly progressive category, as indicated by the comments of people at those companies during many conversations with them. Their managers saw human resources progressiveness as the best way to run a successful business, representing a style and philosophy that are in concert with the times and will enable employees to contribute in the most effective way. They adopted this style voluntarily, not because of pressure or extra money to spend. And it worked, as the evidence presented here strongly supports.

The data from the Survey of Organizations do not prove that human resources progressiveness causes better financial results, but they do prove that the two go hand in hand. The interpretation adopted in this book is that progressiveness causes financial success, rather than the other way around. That is certainly the more logical explanation. But regardless of causation, the important point is that running a company in a way that is in tune with the human resources period simply makes good sense. It enables a company to implement the new technology most effectively and get the most out of the human side of the operation.

4

Alternative Work Styles
in Different Locations

Computers, robots, "smart" machines, and many other technical innovations have completely revamped the workplace in the past few years. As human resources and line managers can readily testify, this explosion in technology has created a tremendous amount of change to be managed. Managers must cope with figuring out which equipment to buy, where to place it, who will use it, and how to train people to become proficient with the new technology.

Significant explosions in technology occurred in our past workplaces as well. The development of machines and mass-production techniques during the industrial revolution altered many aspects of the workplace, as we discussed in Chapter One. Unfortunately, the new technology of the industrial revolution led to a worsening of the work environment for the typical employee. The situation is much brighter in the current workplace revolution, since it potentially offers a vast improvement in working conditions.

This chapter focuses on the *physical workplace* itself. Where will people work? Where will they migrate in order to find the new jobs? The new technology of the human resources period is rapidly changing the location of work itself, and this in turn will affect employee migration patterns. We address these issues from the human as opposed to the engineering or ergonomics perspective, since human resources and line managers need to give full consideration to this perspective to manage change effectively. It is not the technology itself but how that technology affects *employees* that needs to be kept in mind.

Technology and the Workplace

Many new forms of technology affect the workplace today. We consider these not in terms of design or configuration but how they affect employees' job responsibilities and the location of work itself. The use of computers and word processors will become more and more prevalent in the future. There will be very few jobs that do not involve some contact with a computer, and many jobs will involve very extensive work with a computer. Likewise, robots and smart machines will take over increasingly larger amounts of the manufacturing and assembly work now being done by people. The robotic factory is a reality today, and even those operations that cannot be fully automated will be run with relatively few employees. As a simple example, the parent company of a midwestern corn-processing plant that employs 1,200 people recently opened another plant, which is highly automated but performs the same functions. The new plant, which generates more volume than the old one, has fewer than forty employees.

Tremendous advances have also been made in communications devices. Personal computers can be wired to home offices via conventional phone lines. Teleconferencing permits employees to speak to and see each other across the city or across the world. This can now be done over phone lines as well as by satellite transmission. Printers and facsimile machines permit the rapid transfer of information anywhere in the world via computer and either telephone lines or satellite. Through electronic mail, any type of correspondence can be sent and received instantly.

The Survey of Organizations assessed the degree to which companies took advantage of this latest workplace technology. An extraordinary 94 percent of the companies that were high in human resources progressiveness utilized the latest technology, such as robots, state-of-the-art computers, and advanced tele-communications equipment. Only 56 percent of those companies low in human resources progressiveness took advantage of this new technology. These results suggest a link between the use of the latest technology and a company's success, given the correlation of human resources progressiveness with company financial results.

The fact that using the latest technology leads to success is not surprising by itself. But it must be remembered that this success probably results, in part, from relieving employees from boring, repetitive jobs and using them in a more skilled capacity where they are more productive. That is the part that human resources and line managers need to focus on when implementing technology in their companies.

The importance of these technological advances with regard to the physical workplace is that they permit many jobs to be done out of the home. It is no longer necessary for someone to come into a large office to use this technology. Work can return to the home, where it was done for many millions of years before the industrial revolution. The only equipment required for a home work station is a computer terminal, a printer, and perhaps a facsimile machine or telecommunications hookup. This equipment is already available—it is just a matter of setting it up in the home. Currently, there are some four million work stations with complete computer and communications capabilities in offices and homes. Glenn Watts (1983), former president of the Communications Workers of America, estimates that there will be over thirty million such work stations by the year 2000. Certainly, many more of these work stations will be located in the home. That is a likely next step and, as we shall see later, one desirable to both companies and individuals.

Is work at home a realistic option for employees? Would it work for your company? Given the number of people who currently work at home, at least some seven million in the United States, the answer is definitely yes. Among those who work at home right now are salespeople, architects, consultants, therapists, psychologists, teachers, investment counselors, insurance agents, travel agents, accountants, engineers, and lawyers. What these jobs all have in common is that they are white-collar positions, the exact type of job that is growing in numbers and becoming typical during the human resources period. Lower-level positions such as computer technician and technical assistant are also growing and can also be based in the home.

Will employees be less effective in doing their jobs when work is based at home? Studies done in this area, summarized in Gordon and Kelly's (1986) *Telecommuting,* suggest that productivity actually improves rather than deteriorates. As an example of how productivity can be maintained, consider, for example, the job of investment counselor. An investment counselor might perform the following kinds of job tasks: monitoring stock quotations, researching and interpreting company financial results, buying and selling stocks, counseling investors, recommending and initiating investment vehicles such as money markets, bonds, and trusts, and trading information with other investment counselors. Many of these tasks are done by computer, phone, or reference to various publications. These can be done just as easily out of the home as in a downtown office building. The only tasks that present challenges in being done at home are counseling investors and interacting with other investment counselors. But even if these require a face-to-face meeting, there is no reason why this cannot take place at the counselor's home rather than the office, and doing it this way might save the investor some parking expenses and commuting hassles.

In summary, the ability to do the job of investment counselor is not affected by being based in the home. An investment counselor does not need to commute to an office every day to do the bulk of the job tasks. And being home based does not prevent personal meetings with clients or other counselors. These can take place at home, at an office, or via teleconference. If investment counselors of the future go to an office at all, it will probably be because of lack of a computer hookup or mere personal preference on their part.

The same is true of many other jobs in the human resources period. A good number of white-collar and service jobs can be done very effectively from the home with the proper equipment. Be it accountants, programmers, customer service reps, salespeople, or insurance claim processors, all these and people in countless other occupations can move their work into the home. While this movement to the home creates some problems, there are many benefits to outweigh them. The specific costs and benefits of decentralizing the workplace are discussed in the next section.

A Return to the Home

Although *technology* permits work to be done in the home, there are still some potential obstacles to its movement there. Two such obstacles are the costs incurred by companies and employee feelings of isolation. Let us consider the first of these, companies' resistance to paying for work stations in the home. A computer terminal would cost a few hundred dollars, as would a printer. There might also be a monthly charge for a phone hookup for the computer as well as business phone calls. Optional accessories, such as a facsimile machine and teleconference camera and receiver, would add several thousand dollars to the price. Perhaps the company would also provide the employee with a desk and chair. Will companies be willing to pay for this equipment?

Any company that carefully evaluated the costs would provide this basic setup without hesitation. Consider what they are currently spending. First, the company may already be buying computer terminals and printers for its employees to use at the office. Allowing everyone to have them at home would not increase costs. Desks and chairs are already provided at the office, so even if the company provided for these items at home, there would be no extra cost, and perhaps even a savings. Facsimile machines and teleconferencing equipment may already exist at the company, but certainly not for each employee. There would be extra costs here if a firm were to provide them for employee use.

But let us look at the savings incurred by moving work into the home. The company would no longer have to pay:

• The cost of building or renting an office building

- Utility expenses for heating, cooling, and maintaining the office building
- The salaries of maintenance and security people
- Taxes on the building
- The cost of maintenance supplies, such as floor polish, electrical wiring, light bulbs, carpeting, filing cabinets, paint, and wall partitions

Also eliminated would be the company cafeteria and swimming pool, should you be so fortunate as to have these. Companies would also save by not having to "subsidize" commuting. This is done directly by some companies and indirectly by many others. Salary surveys show that the salary paid for the same job will be higher in a large metropolitan city than it will in a suburb of that same city. For example, a secretary in downtown Chicago will earn a few thousand dollars more each year than a person with a comparable position in the far suburbs. One reason for this is the expense of commuting. Employers are providing a subsidy for someone to make a long and expensive commute into the city or live in more expensive city housing.

If employees could work out of their homes, they would accept lower salaries than they demand if they have a long and expensive commute. The net result would be a savings in subsidies for commuting. Even if this amounted to only a few hundred dollars per employee, the employer would save this amount on every employee in the company who decided to work out of the home (this would typically be implemented through attrition). Savings would also be realized in employer taxes on employee wages and benefit costs, since some benefits are linked to pay.

As a result, companies should be glad to move work into the home for the sheer cost savings that are involved. In fact, they would be foolish to pass up the opportunity to increase profits. The expenses for computer terminals and support equipment are trivial in comparison to the expenses for buildings and maintenance costs. And many of the home equipment supplies, such as terminals, are one-time-only costs, whereas building rent and maintenance are annual costs.

Case Study: The NPD Group

The NPD Group is one of the country's largest market research firms. Based in Port Washington, New York, the firm has 800 employees, of whom 200 are involved in some form of data-entry work. NPD decided to consider work at home because of the extremely tight labor market on Long Island and the high cost of commercial buildings and related overhead. Table 6 shows the savings that the firm calculated it would realize by basing 60 of its jobs in the home.

Table 6. Savings from Work at Home: The NPD Group.

Item	Annual Cost at Office	Annual Cost at Home
Equipment lease or depreciation	$ 60,000	$ 30,000
Building and utilities	55,000	0
Labor @ $6/hour	360,000	360,000
Messenger service	0	20,000
Overhead	40,000	20,000
Total	$515,000	$430,000

The cost savings of $85,000 represented a 17 percent reduction. Larger-scale applications could potentially save much more.

NPD uses a "pod" system for supervision of the telecommuters. The employees are divided into groups of twenty, each with its own supervisor, who is also based at home. The supervisors are paid at the same rate as their in-house counterparts and are responsible for providing a "social link" to the employees, day-to-day management, distribution and collection of work, home-office liaison, and administrative tasks, such as hiring, training, and scheduling. The company was surprised that none of its active employees opted to become homebodies when first given the chance. Evidently, there was another breed of employee who wanted this type of work and did not seek out work at the office. After initial advertising, the company developed a waiting list of those who wanted to work out of their homes. Home-based employees are paid on a piece-rate basis, with a guaranteed minimum rate. They receive the same benefits as home-office employees do.

And what are the results? NPD found that employees based at home worked 10–15 percent faster than their counterparts at the office, with no loss in accuracy. The sixty people working at home did the work of eighty at the office. The reasons? Fewer interruptions, the piece rate, and the pod concept are all cited. Whatever the actual reasons, the results are comparable to those of other firms with employees based at home.

Gil Gordon, president of a telecommuting consulting firm, has worked with many firms contemplating or instituting work at home. His work has shown that the old idea "more work, more space" can be broken with work at home—you do not need to keep building or leasing more space every time you add more people. Work at home is a particularly desirable solution for those firms that are growing yet cannot afford to move or lease additional space. Gordon feels that work at home can cut office space needs by 30 percent or more and offers specific case studies of this in his book *Telecommuting* (Gordon and Kelly, 1986). Not only are office space and related utility costs saved, but many firms have leased or subleased the residual office space, resulting in income. Gordon cites studies that have shown productivity increases averaging 20 to 40 percent for people working at home. The reasons for these large gains are the following:

- The ability to work at personal peak times
- Less incidental absence
- Freedom from group productivity norms
- Fewer distractions and interruptions than in the office
- Elimination of the need to leave to catch a certain train, beat the rush hour, or take lunch before eating places become crowded
- More flexible work hours

- Elimination of the need to "recuperate" from the morning commute

Will employees present a possible obstacle to work at home? Perhaps they would prefer to commute to the office every day. It is interesting to speculate about how many people relish a one- to two-hour daily commute into downtown Manhattan from the suburbs in Connecticut. If these employees were given the option of staying at home and merely turning on a computer terminal, how do you think they would choose?

Managers will need to assess the feelings of employees at their companies. Many employees would likely see working at home as a benefit. First of all, commuting expenses as well as wear and tear on the family car would be saved. The aggravation of fighting heavy traffic or waiting in inclement weather for a bus or train would also be eliminated. Meals would be cheaper and probably healthier for many. Then there are the savings in travel time and the advantage of not having to get up as early (or turn in as early) to allow time for commuting. Lastly, work at home might save an employee the price of a few outfits, since business attire will not be as important as in an office.

Another possible objection is that employees might miss the daily interaction with others. But it must be remembered that not *all* work will be done at home. Meetings, training, and other activities will still be carried out at an office. And teleconferencing can be nearly as satisfying as meeting with someone in person. While interactions with co-workers might diminish, the amount of time spent with family members will increase. And that is a nice substitute.

In 1983, there were only 15,000 to 30,000 employees who worked out of their homes with terminals connected to their employers' computers. The number of such "homebodies" working for large firms increased to 100,000 in the next two years, according to Electronic Services Unlimited (1986), a telecommuting consulting firm. That is roughly a 400 percent increase in just two years, and the figures are growing even more dramatically now. By 1990, Electronic Services estimates a few *million* could be based at home or a satellite office (Jack Nilles of the University of Southern California estimates ten million by 1990; see "Working by Wire," 1985).

In addition to those who work for large companies and are based at home, there are many self-employed who work at home. The jobs of seven million consultants, psychologists, journalists, and others are based in the home. These numbers are also increasing rapidly as a result of the growth of service occupations and the entrepreneurial spirit. The net effect is that home-based work is taking on a much greater importance than in the past few hundred years.

It is estimated that 500 medium-sized to large organizations now have at least some employees who work out of their homes. Among the larger ones are the following:

- IBM
- Data General
- GTE
- Aetna
- Hewlett-Packard
- Pacific Bell
- American Express
- Travelers Insurance
- Blue Cross Blue Shield of South Carolina
- City government of Fort Collins, Colorado

The experience of these employers has been very positive. Thomas Faulds, CEO of Blue Cross Blue Shield of South Carolina, feels that work at home is a way to avoid the loss of the eight- to ten-year investment in training when skilled employees leave. Of his company's 1,900 employees, 100 are based at home, and the company is expanding the program. Rick Higgins, project manager for telecommuting at Pacific Bell, mentions that employees are very positive about the work-at-home experience (a study by Electronic Services Unlimited, 1986, showed that 76 percent of homebodies in a number of companies were "somewhat" or "very satisfied" with the experience). Additionally, Pacific Bell was able to shut down a couple of offices by implementing work at home and realized a significant savings. Home-based employees rarely relocated after being based at home, which saved the company significant relocation costs.

The Survey of Organizations assessed the percentage of companies with at least some employees working at home. A total of 40 percent of the companies that were progressive in human resources had employees working out of the home, as opposed to only 8 percent of the less progressive companies. Since human resources progressiveness is related to company financial success, the trend toward work at home bears a relationship to company success. Progressive human resources practices such as work at home lead to better bottom-line results.

The movement back into the home represents coming full circle in our history. For millions of years, the workplace and the home were one and the same. It was only with the industrial revolution that people went to work in factories and offices. They are now returning to where they worked for many generations prior to that time. Perhaps you can go home again after all.

Case Study: Rank Xerox

Rank Xerox of Great Britain undertook an organizational restructuring beginning in 1981 (Judkins, West, and Drew, 1985) because of a need to cut overhead costs. The solution to this problem was "networking," which Judkins, West, and Drew defined as a "system of work in which selected and trained volunteers leave their parent company and found their own business, which then contracts to provide specified services to the parent company among other clients, and uses a microcomputer to do so." Networking was seen as a solution for Rank Xerox because of:

1. *Cost control,* with savings on office space, salaries, salary overhead, and support services—for every £10,000 in salary saved, there was an additional savings of £17,000 pounds on overhead

2. *Self-regulation*—the ability of the professional worker to have more "freedom from detailed managerial supervision"
3. *Technology*—the tools were available to facilitate the networking concept

The work-at-home experience was a great success for Rank Xerox. Not only were costs cut, but key employees were retained and their productivity enhanced. Rank Xerox set up not just a telecommuting process for many of its employees but an entirely new organizational structure to make the process work. Judson, West, and Drew strongly emphasize that such a new organizational structure must be *adaptive* rather than rigid, involve considerably *lower overhead* costs, enhance *creativity,* be *"organic,"* *involve* people, and motivate the production of *quality* work.

Action Steps for the Human Resources or Line Manager

Since work at home is a growing trend and makes sense from the standpoints of costs and employee satisfaction, what should you do about it as a manager? Listed here are some suggested action steps.

A. *Audit your current practices.*
    1. Do any of your employees work out of their homes? If so, how many? What have the results been so far? Learn from experience. If others at your company have already experimented with work at home, take advantage of their successes or make corrections where they failed.
    2. Does your company have available the latest technology to make work at home possible? Consider particularly computer terminals, personal computers, printers, and phone modems. If such equipment is already available, it will probably be possible for people to use it at home. This will save you some of the up-front purchasing costs.

3. Do your plans for the future call for new, large buildings or smaller, decentralized facilities? Are you locked into the new facilities, or is subleasing a possibility? Work at home enables you to save a great deal of office space. You should not expand your facilities at the same time you move some employees into the home.

4. Is your company a growing company? Is space tight, yet you do not want to build or lease a new building? Growing companies with a space shortage will find it particularly advantageous to consider work at home.

5. Are you in an industry where it is easy to implement work at home? The industries that find it easiest to implement work at home are those that involve information-oriented jobs and services, such as consulting firms, software designers, banks, insurance companies, research firms, and training firms.

6. Are you losing more good employees than you would like because of child-care problems, commuting problems, spouse relocations in the same geographical area, or physical disability that is not completely incapacitating? Work at home is a particularly attractive way to retain some of these employees who might otherwise be lost.

7. What jobs do you have that are particularly easy to move into the home? Employees whose jobs are easiest to move into the home are the following:

    - Sales representatives
    - Attorneys
    - Programmers or systems analysts
    - Word processors
    - Data-entry personnel
    - Consultants and counselors
    - Engineers
    - Architects
    - Insurance agents
    - Travel agents
    - Claims processors
    - Training professionals

8. Are your employees interested in work at home? You can pursue work at home regardless of the answer to this question, but you should still survey your employees. If your current work force is interested, transfers may be your solution. If the current work force is not interested (as in the NPD case study), then outside recruiting will be necessary. In this case, you will have to decide whether to add these new people now or as turnover occurs with your office staff.

B. *Put together your proposal and sell it.* If you decide to go forward after the audit, and many companies probably will, here is what to discuss in your final proposal.

1. List exactly which jobs you will experiment with first. In all likelihood, it will not be everyone who holds these jobs who will be transferred, but a certain percentage of incumbents.

2. Address what you will do with the vacated office space. You might move other employees into it or sublease to another tenant.

3. Describe how you will handle supervision for the work-at-home group—whether by supervisors who also work out of their homes and are assigned to people by region or by supervision through the office.

4. Work out a strategy to determine which employees will be offered the opportunity to work at home. Will it be volunteers? Pre-identified people? Outside hires? Your survey of company employees will help you determine this.

5. Determine what home office activities, if any, the work-at-home employees will be encouraged to attend. Training, orientation, occasional staff meetings, and company "events" (picnics, parties) are the most likely.

6. Present the cost and benefit information picture at your company. *Additional expenditures* might include:

   • Miscellaneous supplies (paper, pens, and so on)
   • Phone-line charges

- Recruiting expenses, if telecommuters are not already employed by the company
- Messenger services

Some items that might already be available in house or not be needed are:

- Computer terminals or personal computers
- Printers
- Phone modems
- Facsimile machines
- Desks and chairs
- Teleconference camera and receiver (not likely to be provided)

Cost savings might include:

- Reduced rent for office space
- Reduced utility expenses (heating, cooling, cleaning) for vacated space
- Reduced salaries of maintenance and security personnel
- Tax savings because of reduced square footage
- Savings on maintenance supplies (waxes, wiring, paint)
- Savings on office fixtures (partitions, carpeting, filing cabinets)
- Salary savings if the work-at-home employees live in a less expensive geographical area
- Savings on employer taxes, benefits, and so on from reducing these salaries
- Reduced commuter subsidies (direct or indirect through vans, train discounts, and so on)
- Reduced cafeteria subsidies

If vacated space is leased or subleased, add the rental income. The difference between these cost savings and the additional expenditures determines the value of the program to your company. Most find the savings to be 30 percent or more.

C. *Present your proposal and implement.* If work at home makes sense for your company, present your proposal to senior management. Particularly emphasize the cost savings in your presentation. After selling your ideas and getting approval, implement your plan. Experts in the area suggest making small-scale changes at first so that you can evaluate and adjust where needed. Of particular value would be quantifying productivity and error rates and comparing those of the work-at-home group with those of the office group. Studies suggest that the work-at-home group will do better.

Migration Patterns

Geographical Trends. The human resources period will be best known for returning work to the home, but other types of migration will occur as well. Having work based in the home will greatly increase individual freedom to live in any area desired without worrying about the commute to work. Individuals might opt for the city, the suburbs, or a rural area simply because that is where they prefer to live.

The human resources period should reduce the trend of people moving to where the jobs are, which has been the trend for hundreds of years. Our highly mobile society will become less mobile, except for those who simply like to relocate every few months. With this more stationary population, there should be a much stronger sense of community, since people will get to know their neighbors better. And that will be needed to offset the loss of contact with co-workers that results from work at home. Stronger ties will exist with the community and within the family.

Will employees or companies resist this change to a more stationary life-style? It is highly doubtful, since most people find relocation one of the more traumatic and upsetting experiences in their lives and prefer to remain in an area where they feel that the quality of life best suits them, be that rural, city, or suburban. Companies will probably not resist a reduction in relocations, since they currently spend a great deal of money to move new and existing employees. In a recent year, the average relocation cost per family was roughly $40,000, and the bill came to over $15 billion for the nation as a whole. That is money that companies would rather save than spend.

Movement to the home will not stop relocation entirely. Many employees will want to move to a more desirable area, and some just like to explore and live in different places over the courses of their lives. But we will probably see a great reduction in the number of relocations over the years. For many positions, accepting a new job will simply mean that an employee's home computer terminal is wired to a different employer or that the employee receives new computer equipment from the new employer. That is an easy way to start a new job and is certainly less traumatic than moving everything you own to another part of the country.

If employees have the freedom to live where they wish, what locations will they choose? There is already good evidence that people would like to live in less densely populated areas. Choate (1983) states that many surveys have documented the desire of people to live in areas away from our central cities. The trend for people to move away from the cities actually began in the 1950s, says Choate, and he notes that, while in 1960, 50 percent of the residents of metropolitan areas lived in central cities, the figure in 1980 was only 40 percent, verifying the push away from the central cities.

Before 1970, the growth of metropolitan areas had outpaced that of nonmetropolitan areas for at least 150 years, as far back as accurate records go. During the 1970s, the population of nonmetropolitan areas grew by 15 percent, whereas that of metropolitan areas grew by only 9.5 percent, according to the U.S. Department of Commerce (1975). Of the fifty largest cities in the United States, twenty-nine experienced population *declines* between 1970 and 1980 and only twenty-one experienced increases. Several of our largest cities, including New York, Chicago, Philadelphia, and Detroit, have been steadily declining in population since 1950, when they were at their peak.

In addition to migration away from central cities, there is also regional migration to the South and West of the United

States. This is probably due to a combination of reasons, including better weather, more job availability, and a more favorable business climate. Whatever the exact reasons, there is no mistaking that the movement to the South and West has been dramatic during the human resources period. The population of those regions grew by 21.4 percent during the 1970s, while that of the Northeast and North Central regions grew by only 2 percent. From 1980 to 1986, population in the South and West increased by 13.2 million people (91 percent of the total population increase), while that of the Northeast and the North Central grew by only 1.3 million. More than half (52.3 percent) of the nation's population lived in the South and West in 1980.

Though central cities are declining in population, some cities in the South and West countered the trend. For example, while only twenty-one of the nation's fifty largest cities gained population in the 1970s, twenty of those twenty-one were in the South or West (Columbus, Ohio, was the exception). All twenty-five of the most rapidly growing metropolitan areas in the country are in the South and West—of the thirty-two metropolitan areas that lost population during the 1970s, only two were in the South and West.

Clearly, distant suburbs and rural areas in the South and West offer great hope for growth during the human resources period. Farsighted entrepreneurs will build homes with offices in them in these areas or construct small office places suitable for holding meetings and housing computer and telecommunications equipment. Whether people will still choose to live in the South and West after work moves back into the home is hard to say. Many probably will do so because of the warmer climate, though those not affected by climate may choose to move to areas in the North and Northeast away from the central cities.

There is little doubt that a historic reversal in migration patterns has already begun, and the growth from here on out will be outside of the central cities. The trend will only increase as more people begin to work out of their homes and seek out a more ideal living environment—an environment that in many cases is more open, less congested, and closer to nature than the central cities.

Action Steps for the Human Resources or Line Manager

Human resources and line managers will undoubtedly have to cope with the desire of some employees to live in a different geographical region or outside the central cities. The failure to recognize this trend could cost the loss of valuable employees to competitors with operations in those locations, resulting in additional recruiting expenses, training costs, and productivity losses. Human resources managers in particular will need to take a lead role in analyzing and modifying company practices in this area, since it concerns *employee* location preferences. Here are specific activities you can undertake:

1. Are part of your company's operations currently in the South or West or outside the central cities? Can additional facilities be moved there? Obviously, there are many economic reasons for having offices in certain areas, but you have to consider the "people side" of this issue as well. If you have facilities in the South or West, this will enable you to retain employees who desire to live in these areas by transferring them. Companies with no significant operations in the South or West or outside the central cities may suffer a loss of personnel and find recruiting difficult. Human resources managers need to be the catalysts to identify this problem and promote solutions within their organizations.

2. Can the company's base of operations be moved to the South or West? While an all-at-once move is highly disruptive, a gradual shifting is more easily accommodated. This is particularly true since there is a trend for companies to decentralize (see Chapter Five) and leave behind a lean corporate headquarters. Some companies have established new bases in the South or West without disbanding the original headquarters. For example, Motorola, with headquarters in suburban Chicago, has a large "headquarters" in the Phoenix area. American Express has "triheadquarters" in New York, Fort Lauderdale, and Phoenix. Such a structure permits more flexibility in transferring individual employees or perhaps eventually moving the entire headquarters itself. Human resources managers need to raise and push this issue within their organizations.

3. Do transfer policies make it easy for someone within

your company to relocate? If a company does not provide any financial assistance for moves to other cities, employees could be lost to competitors who *will* fund a move to the South or West. Human resources managers need to ensure that at least some assistance is provided for employee relocations. Greater relocation assistance is typically offered for higher-level jobs as well as for promotions versus lateral moves.

4. Does your company post job openings at all locations? If not, employees interested in a move to the South or West may look outside the company rather than within. It is best to post job openings nationally, at least those above a certain job level, or to implement some other process for employees to identify and apply for jobs outside their immediate area.

Summary

The new technology and new jobs of the human resources period permit many jobs to be based in the home. Companies stand to save a great deal of money by returning work to the home, which is where jobs were based for millions of years before the industrial revolution. Employees will also desire work at home, since it will likely save them commuting time and money. With both companies and employees wanting work at home, there is little to stop this trend, which is accelerating rapidly. The Survey of Organizations confirmed that companies that were progressive in human resources and financially successful were much more likely to use work at home than were less successful companies.

With work moving into homes, employees will have a great deal more freedom in their choice of geographical areas to live in. In the past thirty years, a clear trend has emerged in movement to the South, to the West, and away from the central cities. Successful companies have prepared for this by basing significant operations in the more desirable areas and permitting employees to move to these areas while remaining with the company. We have provided suggestions for human resources or line managers that will help them to ensure that work at home and employee migration will be successfully managed within their companies.

5

Progressive Organizational Structures and Compensation Programs

Just as the physical workplace is changing in the human resources period, so too must the structure of the company itself change. The highly centralized hierarchical structure of the industrial period may be just as inappropriate for the human resources period as it would have been for the agricultural period. Human resources and line managers need to look at their companies' current structure with an open mind and ask whether it really fits the workplace. The failure to adapt can mean a less successful organization, as the Survey of Organizations has already shown.

There are many aspects of company structure that can be reviewed for compatibility, such as department organization, relations between departments, company controls, and operating authority. In this chapter, the focus is on decentralization, levels of management, matrix organization, and compensation systems. These four areas are all greatly affected by the massive change in the workplace today. Each area will be considered in depth with an eye toward designing the company structure so that it is in tune with today's workplace. Specific action steps will be suggested for human resources or line managers to implement in their companies.

Decentralized Operations

The industrial period was characterized by highly centralized operations, a trend that has persisted to this day in many companies. Power and authority were concentrated in a few senior managers, and bigness was a desirable characteristic, be it in corporate headquarters or manufacturing facilities. Much of this stemmed from the mass production of identical goods, it being easier to produce a million widgets at one factory than 10,000 widgets at each of 100 factories. Growing demands for cheap, identical products fueled the creation of large facilities. With these came the need for a centralized structure to manage the large facilities in a tightly controlled, machinelike way. This centralized way of operating is quickly changing. The forces behind this change, which will be reviewed in turn, are the following:

1. Customized products
2. The growth of the service industry
3. Work at home
4. Broader, more generalist jobs
5. Higher employee education and skill levels

The idea of mass producing identical goods is dying out. As Toffler (1980) noted in *The Third Wave,* we are seeing a move toward small runs in production. No longer is the standard product an acceptable one. Both companies and individuals want a product to meet their unique demands. Clothing tailored to fit you perfectly is more desirable than the off-the-rack variety, and a custom-designed piece of furniture is better than mass-produced items.

To date, we have not seen a large number of custom-designed products because the cottage-industry method of production is usually more expensive. But the technology is here that can make custom tailoring quite easy. For example, you might choose a shirt by viewing it on a television screen in your home. The color, the pattern, and your precise dimensions could be selected by computer terminal in the near future. The manufacturing itself can be done by computer-controlled machine and yet not cost significantly more than the manufacture of hundreds of identical copies.

A recent report of the National Research Council's Manufacturers Studies Board (1987) noted a trend toward a "proliferation of smaller factories closer to final markets.'' It further stated, ''For some industries, the concept of the microfactory will become important: Small factories, highly automated and with a specialized, narrow product focus, would be built near major markets for quick response to changing demand.'' Once this type of customizing becomes commonplace, the large manu- facturing facility and the large office that goes with it will be unnecessary. The local branch production facility will be more than adequate, without a need for highly centralized control.

It must also be remembered that the products of the human resources period are more likely to be services than material goods. The services lend themselves very naturally to customizing. It is hard to think of an accountant helping prepare a tax return, or an attorney helping with a legal problem, without taking into consideration the individual's unique needs. Since white-collar and service jobs will predominate throughout the human resources period, so too will decentralized, small facilities rather than large, centralized ones. The decentralized facilities make it easier to adapt services and products to the local con- sumer. Large centralized operations would only get in the way.

Another very strong factor that will cause decentraliza- tion is the return of work to the home, as discussed in Chapter Four. The large office or factory does not serve any useful pur- pose when employees are based in their homes. Such buildings are merely assets to be disposed of for whatever financial gain can be obtained. While small conference centers, computer centers, and training facilities will all have their place in the human resources period, the megastructures will perhaps be- come monuments to an earlier era, as the following illustration indicates.

Case Study: Potential White Elephants?

The real estate industry is known for its cyclicality, hav- ing had both good and bad periods in the past twenty years. In the mid to late 1980s, an oversupply of office buildings ex- isted in every major metropolitan area. Vacancy rates ranged from 10 percent to over 20 percent. Many investments have gone bad, and many developers have gone bankrupt. The Southwest, faced with a slump in the oil industry during this period, was particularly hard hit. Houston and Dallas have become known for their "transparent" office buildings, so named because the windows could be seen straight through, since there were no tenants.

With the growth of the work-at-home movement, and decentralizing becoming a way of life, large office buildings would seem to be needed less and less. Will the most recent or a future slump in the commercial real estate industry be more than just a brief cycle? Which is the best choice for future development, large office buildings or small mini-offices outside the central cities—mini-offices that can house computer and telecommunications equipment and provide meeting rooms at a fraction of the size and cost of today's large office buildings? Only the future will tell.

The last two factors influencing decentralization are the evolution of generalist jobs and the higher education and skill levels of the work force. Generalist jobs (see Chapter Seven) allow for greater decentralization, since employees holding such jobs are capable of performing a wide variety of tasks. They can operate more autonomously and can therefore be based in a decentralized location. The more independent, complex, and creative nature of generalist jobs also means that close supervision and tight, centralized control are less necessary. The net result is greater ability to decentralize.

Closely associated with the growth of generalist jobs is the increase in education and skills of the work force. Employees want to put these additional education and skills to good use. They will therefore be attracted to and more productive in generalist types of jobs that permit a great deal of growth and autonomy. Decentralized facilities *require* this type of job and will put these skills to good use. The net result is that the more skilled work force will be better capable of handling generalist jobs, and that will permit more decentralization.

The movement to decentralize is already well under way. Many companies proudly speak of the highly decentralized nature of their operations. Examples include the Hyatt organization and the Marmon Group, both owned by the Pritzker family, Northwest Industries (and its acquirer, Farley Industries), and Beatrice Companies. Such companies emphasize the benefits of local management autonomy and keep very lean corporate staffs. As time goes on, more and more companies will need to adapt to this style to be as productive as possible. The failure to accommodate will be costly for companies that continue to use old, industrial-period structures.

Case Study: The Decentralized Computer Company

Many of the leading computer companies (IBM, Hewlett-Packard, Tandem, Apple, Prime) are similarly structured in that they are all highly decentralized. These companies include in their operating philosophy the goal to delegate responsibility and decision making to the lowest possible level. Corporate leadership activity is restricted to determining the general direction of the company and its products and services. Even here, input from the field is highly sought after.

The typical computer company structure has a corporate headquarters overseeing divisional, regional, district, and branch offices, each with a correspondingly smaller geographical territory. Each office, regardless of place in the hierarchy, has responsibilities for sales, customer service, and technical systems support. The managers of these functions at the local level are free to manage the business on their own, calling upon the larger offices only when additional support or technical expertise is needed. The managers are held accountable for results, and there is no undue interference in local operations.

These computer companies have even decentralized administrative staff functions, which are notoriously centralized at many companies. Functions such as accounting, purchasing, leasing, human resources, and even legal activities operate at the lowest level possible. There is not necessarily an accountant, human resources professional, or attorney at each branch, which might have only ten to fifteen employees, but these positions might be included at the district or regional level where the size of the operation would justify a full-time person.

The push to decentralize is not unaccompanied by some debate and head scratching at these companies. Should a company, for example, decentralize a human resources data base, allowing small offices to change salaries at the local level? A decentralized operating style would suggest that this be done without question, but many issues need to be dealt with, such as training someone to perform this infrequent task at the local level, providing the necessary equipment, and providing checks and security around the data. Maybe this is better kept centralized, given the inherent problems. The answer is not a simple yes or no, but in general these companies have tried to decentralize as much as possible, even when there are some complications. It is a deeply ingrained operating style that they believe leads to success. And our survey results also suggest that operating this way leads to success.

Is the typical company decentralized now? That question was asked in the Survey of Organizations, and the results showed that decentralizing was quite common. Companies that were high in human resources progressiveness reported being *very* decentralized in 82 percent of all cases. Those low in human resources progressiveness reported being very decentralized in 62 percent of all cases. While most companies described themselves as very decentralized, the trend was stronger among those who were more progressive, and these same companies enjoyed much better financial results than their less progressive counterparts. Decentralizing is related to the bottom line.

Action Steps for the Human Resources or Line Manager

Decentralizing the workplace requires a significant effort on the part of many employees. Specific actions that can be taken to accomplish this are as follows:

1. Analyze your company's present structure. Is it highly centralized, decentralized, or somewhere in between? Most highly successful companies push toward decentralization wherever possible, and the remaining steps are based on the assumption that you wish to do the same.

2. Form a task force that has decentralizing as its sole mission. Members of the task force should include senior managers as well as more junior people from each of the major functional areas in your company.

3. Analyze the controls the company currently has in place. Where are decisions made? Where must you go for approval on purchases or additional personnel? Are corporate policies strictly enforced, or is local autonomy allowed? By answering such questions, you will better understand your current situation and where you want to be. Draw up a list of the activities that might be decentralized, such as:

- Adding to or reducing personnel
- Entering into contractual relationships with clients
- Making purchases, leases, or modifications to offices
- Running a profit and loss center
- Carrying out marketing activities
- Negotiating prices on products or services provided

4. Decide how far each activity on your list can be decentralized. Be prepared for lengthy discussions in this area. Work up a final summary of the consensus position for each item.

5. You must review your current staff capabilities when deciding to decentralize. For example, if local branch managers will be given the added authority to negotiate leases and contracts, what are their capabilities to do this? Additional training might be needed, and perhaps even a different caliber of manager. Plan and implement these activities before you decentralize. Also consider what will happen to some of the corporate staff and the related office space. Will you transfer people to the field or terminate their employment? These actions need to be planned in advance as well.

The "Flattened" Hierarchy

"Flattened management hierarchies"—that is, management structures with few supervisory levels—are becoming the norm during the human resources period. One of the reasons for the drive toward a flattened hierarchy is changes in the nature of jobs. The new jobs of the human resources period (discussed more fully in Chapter Seven) are white-collar and service occupations that are more generalist oriented and require more skills than jobs of the past. They also involve more shared responsibilities and teamwork than before. What these new jobs have in common is that they *require* less supervision—highly skilled, white-collar generalists are capable of handling many activities on their own.

If less direct supervision is needed, then each manager can potentially supervise a greater number of employees. A flat management hierarchy, with a larger number of direct reports, is a good fit for the jobs of today. A large number of hierarchical levels and tight management controls would also interfere with shared responsibilities and teamwork.

Another factor contributing to a flattened hierarchy is the movement toward fewer policies and rules. During the industrial period, every aspect of employee performance was closely monitored for adherence to tight rules and procedures. There was a right way and a wrong way to do each job. This emphasis on tight control and an overabundance of work rules required close supervision. But the human resources period will strip away many of those work rules and leave only those that are absolutely necessary. Supervision will be less controlling, meaning that each supervisor can supervise more people. Once again, that allows for a flattened hierarchy.

The increased decentralization of companies will also contribute to a more flattened hierarchy. With responsibility and autonomy pushed downward, mid-level and senior managers can manage a larger number of people. The emphasis will be on small, autonomous operations tailored to the local customer. Many layers of management would only get in the way.

One last, and very important, factor in the move toward

a flattened hierarchy is the related cost savings. As many companies have already discovered, eliminating unnecessary middle-management levels can save significant amounts of money, not only in salaries but also in employee benefits, office space, furniture, utilities, and other related costs.

According to *Fortune* magazine (cited in Zemke, 1987), between 1981 and 1983, half of the 1,000 largest companies in this country eliminated at least one level of management. General Motors and Chrysler eliminated three levels, and Ford eliminated five. This type of action appears to increase the pressure on the remaining managers. In a recent survey by Zemke (1987), 54 percent of the respondents felt that their managers were under increased stress in the past few years. A total of 48 percent reported that their managers worked more hours than before, and 25 percent said that their managers had to regularly work weekends just to keep up. One-third of the respondents felt that their managers were near the burnout level. This is especially likely if the managers are not practicing participative management techniques and not delegating where they should. With an appropriate management style (see Chapter Ten) and the correct structure for jobs, the flattened hierarchy itself should not cause increased management pressure.

Gunther Klaus, managing director of the Institute for Advanced Planning in Beverly Hills, California, has been a keen observer of the new flattened hierarchy. In a recent essay, he observed that ''The traditional managerial pyramid is being subjected to the wrecker's ball. An almost flat horizontal organization structure is emerging, signaling enormous change for the 21st century'' (Klaus, 1983, p. 56). Klaus feels that management trends in Japan, such as the consensus decision making of the Ringi system, have triggered much of the movement toward a flattened organization.

Klaus cites an engineering consulting firm in California as an example of the highly flattened organization. The firm has only two ranks and two pay scales: vice-presidents making $65,000 per year and associates making $35,000 per year. Even the switchboard operator and cafeteria cook are considered associates and receive the corresponding pay. While that may be an extreme example, it is indicative of the trend that is occurring.

The flat management hierarchy is clearly the appropriate structure for companies of the human resources period. By minimizing the levels of management and the closeness of supervision, companies can allow employees to more fully perform the jobs of this period, making for more satisfied employees. It is interesting to recall that employees worked in flat organizations for our entire history up until the industrial revolution. We are coming full circle.

Case Study: Flat and Very Flat Hierarchies

Companies such as Ralston Purina, Eaton, and Cummins Engine have experimented with "self-managed" production teams for several years. Such concepts are now becoming more ingrained in the fabric of American business. Two interesting examples of flat hierarchies and participative employee programs come from the automobile industry—a domestic Nissan plant and a Dana truck axle plant.

Nissan recently built one of the most highly automated plants in the world in Smyrna, Tennessee. The plant was originally built to manufacture small trucks but was later converted to manufacture automobiles. All employees at the plant, including Nissan U.S.A. president Marvin Runyon, wear the same blue uniforms, park in the same parking lot, and eat in the same cafeteria. The Nissan plant in Smyrna has only five levels of management, from the lowest-level "technician" to the company president. That contrasts with the typical ten to twelve levels of management found in most American auto plants.

Nissan organized its technicians into teams of from eighteen to twenty people. Instead of each employee knowing only specialized tasks, all employees rotate and learn everyone else's job. Jobs are seen as a group effort, much as barn raising was seen by farmers. Collaborative team efforts are encouraged, and decisions are made by consensus. Gone are the many levels of close supervision and antiquated work rules that are typical at many other companies.

Dana Corporation operates a heavy axle division in Hilliard, Ohio. The plant recently had $150 million in sales and 125 production employees. None of these employees punched a time clock or reported to a foreman. Dana set up the plant so that employees were their own managers and were, in essence, supervised by no one. Employees were put on salary and told that how hard they work and what methods they use would be up to them. At Dana Hilliard, there is no supervisory hierarchy at all. There are no levels of supervision to be found.

Steve Cobb, plant manager when the plant first opened, asked the question, "Why do we need to have a supervisor? More times than not, they end up being policemen walking up and down aisles to make certain that people are working" (personal communication, June 1987). Dana created an environment where all employees cooperated in establishing and working toward common objectives. Employees were selected very carefully and, as at Nissan, rotated to different jobs so that they understood the entire production process. Cobb concluded that "80 to 90 percent of the people do enjoy that freedom and the ability to make decisions. They're looking to improve and, hopefully, they're looking at this as their business." When a climate such as this can be established, with broader jobs, few rules, and a decentralized philosophy, the flattened hierarchy works just fine. In Dana's case, that went as flat as can be, with no levels of supervision.

The Matrix Organization. Going hand in hand with the flat management hierarchy is the matrix organization. A matrix organization is one in which reporting relationships are kept flexible, and individuals (or functions) may simultaneously report to multiple areas or to different areas for different projects. Matrix organizations have enjoyed much success of late, and their use is growing. Shell Oil Company's chemical group was one of the early pioneers of the matrix organization, paving the way for other companies. In 1970, Shell's chemical business had six operating groups, each of which had its own staff. As one manager said, "We had six of everything." They converted to a matrix style of reporting relationships and reduced the repetition in staffing. Over the next eight years, sales tripled with no increase in staff.

Matrix organizations give companies the flexibility to adapt to rapidly changing conditions. At many companies, technology, products, and services are changing so rapidly that the revised organization chart is out of date before the ink is dry. With a matrix set up, employees can report to whomever they need to for as long as they need to. While there are some anxieties created by a matrix system ("Who do I report to?"), the benefits to a company would seem to outweigh the problems.

Action Steps for the Human Resources or Line Manager

Presented below are specific actions that can be taken to implement a flat hierarchy.

1. Audit your current number of supervisory levels. How many levels of supervision are there between the CEO and the lowest-level employee? Between the heads of various functional groups and their lowest-level employees? How many people typically report directly to your managers? Are the trends consistent at your company, or do they differ by functional area? If they differ, is there a good reason for this?

2. Implement a flatter hierarchy if you need this. There are many human resources issues to be considered during this process. For example, you will need to internally place or outplace the managers whose positions are eliminated. If implementation is gradual, attrition may take care of many of these problems. The new structure and philosophy will need to be communicated to employees. Their help will be needed in implementing the change.

When the structure for a flatter hierarchy is decided upon, job design must be thought out. More responsibility and authority will need to be delegated to employees, since managers cannot manage the same amount of detail when they supervise greater numbers of people. Those being supervised should be trained to take on additional responsibility before the new structure is implemented.

Similarly, managers need to practice participative management when supervising a large number of employees. There simply will not be enough time for involvement in every decision and review of every detail. If managers are not prepared for this, they will suffer great stress or operate ineffectively after the transition is made.

3. Relieve some of the burdens on management wherever you can when changing to a flatter hierarchy. Do away with needless rules and policies that eat away at precious time. Minimize the administrative paperwork unless it is absolutely essential.

4. Build a sense of teamwork among peers. Train and encourage them to self-manage and informally manage each other. That will help provide relief to the managers. In addition, have peers rotate jobs so that they can more easily cover for each other, instead of a manager having to fill in when a job is vacant.

Structuring Compensation Programs

Many companies have failed to structure a link between an employee's job performance and his or her pay. This trend started in the industrial period and has persisted to the present time for many employers. Yankelovich and Immewahr (1983) found that 45 percent of the work force believed that there was no relationship between their performance and their pay. In fact, only 13 percent felt that they would personally benefit by working harder and more effectively. "Others," such as the company, were seen as the benefactors of increased effort, rather than the employee. Many even felt that they would be punished for working harder, through the loss of overtime pay or even the loss of a job.

Compensation practices are responsible for many of these feelings. Consider, for example, the typical union contract. In many cases, starting wages are identical for all employees in the same job. Once a year, or at some other set time, employees receive the same amount of pay increase. These increases are a function of time, not performance. Whether the employee is a superstar or a bit below average, the pay increase is the same (very poor performers, of course, would be dismissed from the company). And many of these employees lack any profit sharing, bonus, or individual incentive plans. So where is the motivation to work harder? Many have said, "Why put out extra effort when it never leads to anything?"

The same situation holds true for many companies that do not have union contracts. In some companies, the same general increases might be given to all, or the difference between merit increases for the superstar and the average performer might be insignificant, perhaps only 2 percent in times of low inflation. This difference has little motivational impact. As an example, if two employees were each earning $20,000 per year, the superstar who receives a 2 percent greater increase than the average employee would gross $7.69 (maybe a bit over $5.00 after taxes) more per week than the average employee. Incentive for more effort? Not likely, unless some other incentive programs are in place.

Many of the jobs in the human resources period will themselves provide a source of motivation for employees, since much of the work will be challenging and stimulating. However, pay should not be discounted as a motivator, since employees have financial needs and are interested in improving their financial status.

Pay can serve as a source of motivation and job satisfaction only when there is a clear link between performance and pay (Lawler, 1971, provides an excellent summary of studies in this area). Nearly two out of three employees today want to see pay more closely tied to performance (Yankelovich and Immewahr, 1983). This suggests that companies should abandon their fixed salary structures and replace them with systems that significantly reward employees for their contributions.

The Survey of Organizations found a strong correlation between paying for performance and company success. It was found that 86 percent of the highly progressive and financially successful companies described their salary increases as *definitely* being based on performance, while only 30 percent of the less progressive companies based their salary increases on performance. This evidence strongly suggests that paying for performance is associated with running a financially successful company. Below we consider the key elements of an effective compensation system:

- Merit increase philosophy
- Salary range adjustments
- Stock incentive systems
- Short-term rewards
- Praise

Merit Increases. The merit increase philosophy is perhaps the most important element of an effective compensation system for companies of the human resources period. Company culture and policy must strongly emphasize the concept of "pay for performance"—the more effectively someone performs, the greater the merit salary increase. This philosophy must be communicated to all employees and job applicants, described in detail during new employee orientation programs, and practiced by all managers.

Merit increase guidelines that reflect the pay-for-performance concept should be distributed to and known by all managers. Employees should also know what their salary increases can be for different levels of performance. This means that there must be open communication to all on how the merit increase system works. Performance appraisal programs are also necessary, for if you want to link performance and pay, you must first know what performance is. Appraisals that reflect the achievement of goals will be particularly effective.

Salary Range Adjustments. Many companies of the industrial period adjust their salary ranges annually to ensure competitiveness, basing the adjustments on salary surveys and implementing them through a formal, structured process. While that type of adjustment process may have worked in the industrial period, it will not work as effectively now. The pace of change is too quick for formal, annual adjustments.

As technology is changing rapidly, so too are job responsibilities. New jobs may be created that did not exist six months ago. Others undergo rapid change that makes them vastly different. There may be a paucity of skilled employees in some areas, rapidly driving salaries up, and a surplus in other areas, driving salaries down. All of these rapid market changes render ineffective the formal, once-a-year adjustments to salary ranges. Companies that stick to such practices may find themselves losing good talent to other companies and being unable to attract outside candidates.

The related practice of rejecting outstanding job candidates because "the company has a practice of not hiring people above midpoint" is also ineffective in the human resources period.

Simply put, the solution to adjusting ranges in rapidly changing times is for the company's practices to be market driven. Let the marketplace determine what the going rate is for a given job and pay accordingly. Adjust the salary ranges upward or downward for particular jobs whenever the need arises, not just once a year. Let salary ranges be in a constant state of change to reflect what is taking place in the job market. These are the practices used by the highly progressive and successful companies that were surveyed. They are in tune with the human resources period.

Stock Ownership. The Survey of Organizations found that the degree of employee stock ownership in companies today depends on the type of organization. Of those companies that were high in human resources progressiveness, a remarkable 96 percent encourage their employees to own stock in the company. As a result, over 50 percent of their employees actually do own company stock. Of those companies low in human resources progressiveness, only 56 percent encourage their employees to own stock, and company shares are held by only 20 percent of their employees. Since human resources progressiveness is strongly linked to company financial performance, the results verify that building employee ownership in the company is related to the success of the company.

Successful companies allow their employees to purchase stock at a discount. This builds identification with the company's overall success and profitability. If the employee owns a piece of the firm, the difficulties in making a profit or attracting investors are better understood. The employee also shares in the rewards or suffers when times are bad. In either case, the individual identifies more strongly with the organization than when no stock is owned.

Companies of the future will go further than mere stock purchase. For example, long-term stock options might be given to employees at the time of hire or for outstanding performance. While industrial companies have done this for some executive positions, successful companies will do so for all job levels. A recent survey by Balkin and Gomez-Mejia (1985) found that 55 percent of all high-tech companies offered long-term stock options to key contributors and 27 percent gave out long-term stock awards. Such stock options are effective because they build identification with the company, serve as an effective reward, do not cost much up front, since they are based on long-term results, and make the company more resistant to takeovers, since employees own a significant part of the company.

Short-Term Rewards. The discussion on structuring compensation has thus far focused on longer-term incentives, such as merit pay. However, there is also a need for short-term rewards for special, one-time employee achievements of short duration, such as working three successive weekends to complete a major proposal or referral of a key prospect by an employee who is not in a sales position. Short-term rewards should be available to recognize this type of performance when it occurs.

The successful companies examined in our survey used short-term rewards for these achievements. One such reward was a "night on the town" for the employee and a spouse or friend, with the company paying for dinner at a good restaurant, the theater or a sports event, and a stay at a local hotel. Other rewards included plaques or certificates, small amounts of stock, gift certificates, or small amounts of cash. All such rewards are an unexpected surprise and add something not provided by long-term rewards.

Praise. This is perhaps one of the easiest and least expensive rewards to give out, yet it is often overlooked. Praise for a job well done goes a long way toward satisfying esteem needs. In many cases, verbal reinforcement can mean as much as a gift of some sort. While many would agree that this should be an important part of structuring a compensation strategy, the trick is to have managers practice it on an ongoing basis. Companies progressive in human resources are able to build a culture where this is done all the time.

Employee praise will probably increase in importance, and be more difficult to administer, in the human resources period. One reason for this is that supervisor-employee interactions will be less frequent with many jobs based in the home. Praise in front of a group and face to face will be quite limited. Managers will need to be trained and highly skilled in using praise effectively and taking advantage of all opportunities for providing such feedback.

Case Study: Heller Financial

Heller Financial is a commercial financial services company that makes loans to businesses for a wide variety of purposes. The company has been in business for nearly sixty years and has 1,700 employees in the United States and more than 1,000 overseas. Heller's compensation practices were not very progressive. Bonuses were used for only a handful or so of the very senior managers. There were no incentive plans except for the relatively small sales force. Compensation was a well-guarded secret, with only the senior managers and a few people in human resources knowing the salary ranges and policies. While a merit increase system was being used, employees were never told what the guidelines were; they knew only the amount of their actual increases. Job evaluation and the setting of salary ranges were conducted formally, with the ranges increased once a year.

Heller was purchased by Fuji Bank of Japan in 1984. With this purchase came a new senior management team, which desired to revamp many programs, including compensation. The following changes were all implemented within a year's time.

First, the company adopted a "pay-for-performance" philosophy, which was emphasized to all employees through a special program and described to job candidates during the application process and to new hires during orientation. The chairman reinforced the idea in his monthly newsletter to employees.

Second, communication about compensation was to be open. Employees were given copies of the salary ranges for all job grades except very senior positions (these very senior positions were not graded with ranges in the traditional sense). Employees were also given the merit increase guidelines so that they would know how performance appraisal ratings translated into suggested salary increases. Questions were actively encouraged in open forums. Pay was no longer to be a secret.

Third, incentive systems were put in place for every employee in the company. All managers were eligible for some type of bonus, ranging from 10 percent of salary for the lowest-level managers to over 50 percent for the highest-level managers. Sales representatives continued to have an incentive plan, though it was extensively revamped to make it more effective.

Every employee outside of management and sales was eligible for two incentive plans, a profit-sharing plan and an operations incentive plan. Under the profit-sharing plan, the company contributed up to 6 percent of each employee's salary to a special account. The exact amount contributed was determined by the degree of attainment of *companywide* financial goals that were known to all in advance. Each employee could choose among several different ways for the money to be invested.

The operations incentive plan provided for a cash payout to each employee every six months. The amount of money actually paid out was a function of how well the employee's *business unit* met its goals for that six-month period and was the same for each employee in the unit.

Finally, Heller changed its salary adjustment practices to be market driven. The grading and related salary range for a given job were based on what the market said the job was worth. Adjustments could be made at any time.

Employee reactions to the new compensation system were very positive, as was verified by group meetings, informal feedback, and periodic job attitude surveys. The Heller Financial experience shows that compensation practices can be dramatically changed in a short period of time.

Action Steps for the Human Resources or Line Manager

To ensure that your company is structuring compensation programs effectively, the following action steps should be taken:

1. Start by evaluating how closely you link pay to performance. Is this idea a part of your company's culture and operating philosophy? Are salary increases based on merit or on length of time in the job? Is there a bonus system? Are all employees in your company on some sort of incentive system? Is stock ownership strongly encouraged? Are salary range policies and guidelines communicated to all, or just to managers?

2. Once you have decided on the elements of your pay-for-performance program, openly communicate them to your employees. Hold open-forum meetings to share the information and actively encourage questions. Holding back information will only breed suspicion and mistrust. The pay-for-performance philosophy must also be openly espoused by your managers. If necessary, incorporate these ideas into your management development programs. In addition, mention your practices in recruiting brochures and in interviews with job candidates and describe them thoroughly at orientation programs for new hires.

3. At the very least, set up a merit increase system for all of your employees. Ensure that the increases given to outstanding performers are significantly greater than those given to average performers and that employees are aware of this. Set up incentive systems for all employees, not just managers and

sales representatives. Incentives should be linked to company or business unit results so that employees develop a team perspective and understand the importance of the company's overall success. Share financial results periodically so employees can track progress toward the established incentive goals.

4. Stock purchases and options should be made available within the company. Minimally, allow employees to purchase stock at a discount so they have the pride of ownership and can follow company trends in the market. Preferably, set up a stock option program with a long time, perhaps three years, to vest. Offer these stock options at the time of hire and as periodical performance rewards for key contributors. Design the plan so that these options are available throughout the company, not just to senior managers.

5. Set up programs for smaller, short-term rewards, such as a night on the town, a gift certificate, or a share of stock, to recognize a job well done. Through training and performance appraisal, ensure that managers are praising effective job performance. This free reward is often one of the easiest to forget when formal incentives are in place.

6. Let your company's salary ranges be driven by market conditions. Build flexibility into the compensation program and avoid the "we can't give an offer above midpoint" mentality. If an offer above midpoint is what it takes to get a good performer, adjust your compensation system to the market reality.

Summary

This chapter has described ways of structuring the company for maximum effectiveness in the human resources period. Decentralization is an important part of this structuring. Responsibilities and accountabilities will be assigned to the lowest levels of the hierarchy possible. More highly skilled and effectively trained employees will be sought to operate successfully in a decentralized environment. Financially successful companies in our survey have been following these practices for several years now.

Another practice that the financially successful companies have undertaken is instituting a flat management hierarchy. This is compatible with both the new jobs of the human resources period and decentralizing efforts. Managers must delegate and be participative to prevent work overload in a flat hierarchy.

Finally, we addressed the structuring of compensation systems. In this area, highly progressive companies pay for performance, openly communicate their policies, base salary ranges on market conditions, and use a variety of incentives such as bonuses and stock options for all employees. All of these practices contribute to better sales and profits for companies.

6

Building an
Effective Culture

Peopl e are our most important asset," says the company annual report. For some organizations, those are merely empty
words that sound nice but are not translated into practice. Other
companies have an operating style and philosophy that immediately tell you that people *are* the most important asset. They
practice this day in and day out in a wide variety of ways. As
was shown earlier, companies that have these progressive human
resources practices are more financially successful than those
that do not. And to be successful from here on out, a company
must emphasize the importance of human resources.

Why are human resources the most important asset? Employees today are not as easily replaced as they once were. Jobs
are becoming more complex, skill requirements increasing, and
training taking longer. Companies make a substantial investment
in developing fully qualified employees. No longer can you plug
in a replacement employee like a piece of machinery, as was
done in the industrial period. Turnover and lost productivity
have driven home the value of human assets to a company.

In addition, service organizations do not have the investment in physical assets that manufacturing companies did. No
longer are warehouses, product inventory, real estate, and raw
materials as important as they once were. The only significant
assets are *people,* unless you want to count desks and chairs. And
those human assets must be managed more carefully than physical assets, since replacing them is so difficult.

Another reason why human resources are an important asset is that the products of service organizations are not material goods but services provided by *people*. Attorneys, consultants, psychologists, and technicians all provide information and assistance; eliminate the employee and you have no product. Even in manufacturing organizations, the value of people has gained in importance since most manufacturing is now less labor intensive. The jobs that remain have a much greater impact on the bottom line. A company will not have a leading product unless it has effective technicians, salespeople, customer service representatives, and staff support people. The human side of the equation for success has increased in value for all types of organizations.

If people are the most important asset in a company, what kinds of practices and programs can the human resources or line manager set up to emphasize the importance of human resources? The solution is much more than a sentence in the annual report stating that people are an important asset. There must be a complete culture that manifests this idea. Both the formal and informal culture, made evident through company management practices, programs, and policies, must support the idea that people are an important asset. The daily operating style must reinforce the importance of human resources to the company's success.

Are companies building a culture with a strong emphasis on people? The Survey of Organizations assessed this question, and, once again, dramatic differences were found between companies. Of those companies high in human resources progressiveness, an amazing 90 percent had a company culture that strongly emphasizes people. Only 20 percent of the less progressive companies had such a culture. Since the highly progressive companies had much better financial results than the less progressive, establishing a strong culture pays off in the form of a company's financial success. There was a definite relationship between a strong human resources emphasis and better sales and profits.

The need for such a culture goes beyond attaining better financial results. Everyone has needs for affiliation, needs to be a part of the team. With a strong emphasis on people, employees can have this sense of commonality with others who work at the same company. As members of a team, employees will feel that they have a common mission and goals and will work together to attain those goals. These affiliation needs are going to be more difficult to fulfill in the future, with many jobs returning to the home, where contact with others is limited.

Toffler (1980) notes the recent rise of cults, which he states are growing because of an increasing sense of loneliness and the need for meaning and "community" in people's lives. The company culture, when strong enough, can be a "cult" of sorts and provide this sense of meaning and affiliation for employees. An employee of a computer company that finished in the top twenty in our survey once told me that upon starting with the company, he felt he was "joining a cult, not a company." Indeed, if the culture is as strong as it was at this company, these are the positive feelings that result. Given the time and effort people spend working in their lives, that sense of culture is important to build.

Human resources and line managers have a key role in building the company culture. While the specifics will differ from company to company, the general theme, of course, has to be that employees are the most important asset. It starts with the CEO expressing this and meaning it, as Thomas Watson did at IBM when he said that their most important value as a company was "respect for the individual." The key components of an effective company culture are as follows:

1.   Company mission and goals
2.   The work climate
3.   Management style
4.   Company policies and practices
5.   Hiring and career development
6.   Pay and benefits practices

This chapter offers specific suggestions for developing each of these components to be in tune with the workplace of the future. These suggestions should be tailored to the particular needs of each company. A company's statement of its culture should reflect only those ideas that it actually practices. If a company desires to change its current practices, the statement can include such wording as "we want to become . . ." Ideas on how to communicate and reinforce the derived culture are discussed later in this chapter.

Components of Company Culture

Company Mission and Goals. The culture of a company should express what the company is all about, what its mission is. For example, what types of business is the company in? Which types will be the most important in the future? What makes the company different from its competitors? Is it the most cost-effective? The largest? The fastest growing? The highest-quality producer? The most customer oriented? All such company themes have implications for human resources. If a company wants to be the highest-quality producer, then employees will perform with that idea in mind. If it wants to be the most customer oriented, then employees will focus on that idea. If nothing is said about the company theme and mission, employees will not strive for any particular ideal.

Company goals are another important part of the culture that all employees should be aware of. If the company goal is to increase sales by 30 percent or have the top quality rating in the industry, or attain profit margins of 8 percent, then *everyone* in the organization has a role in helping attain that goal. Many companies stop communicating specific goals at the management level and hope that the idea will trickle down to the lower levels, which often does not happen. A sense of teamwork, unity, and belonging occurs only if everyone pulls on the rope in the same direction. However, employees cannot do this unless they know what the goals are. The goals must be communicated to all with a "linking pin" idea—that "we are all in this together" and have to work together to attain the goal.

Case Study: The Culture at Tandem Computers

Does knowing the mission and goals have any value for lower-level employees? Let me cite two simple examples from personal experience I had at Tandem Computers. On one occasion, as I waited outside the office of one of the company's managers, I overheard the conversation of two administrative assistants on the other side of a seven-foot partition, who were not aware of my presence. They were discussing the preparation of a sales proposal that contained some new material as well as some "boilerplate" that was photocopied from an earlier proposal, and the photocopied part of the proposal did not look as crisp and clear as the rest. One employee said to the other, "That's not Tandem's way of doing things. We want a high-quality result, so I think we should redo the proposal." They did redo the proposal, and it came out looking perfect.

Another such incident took place at a company social event, where I was talking with a customer engineer whose job it was to repair computers. He told me that the company usually discarded computer boards that were not functioning properly because it was costly and time-consuming to find and replace individual computer chips on the board that were flawed. However, he was putting in some of his evenings and weekends to refurbish these boards for use again. When I asked him why he was doing this, he replied, "It saves money and will help us attain our goal of 18 percent pretax profit." He quoted that figure just as easily as his phone number, and it was indeed the company's profit goal for that year.

The customer engineer and the administrative assistants were all in lower-level jobs with Tandem. Yet they had a very clear understanding of the company's mission and its goals. This is very rare for employees in these types of jobs. In some firms, even senior-level managers do not know where the company is going. The payoff for building a strong culture is that employees work, often unnoticed, toward the attainment of the company's goals—even very low-level employees. That is the type of environment all managers would like to have, and it *can* be done.

The Work Climate. Company culture is also determined by the work climate. One important aspect of work climate is company communication, which serves to set the operating tone for the company. For example, hold back on sharing information with employees, and suspicion and mistrust will result. Have a great many closed-door meetings, and secrecy and rumors will result. Each manager in some way contributes to the climate that is set through communications.

Companies in tune with the human resources period will openly share information with their employees. The information shared should include company profits, goals, problems, and policies as well as general announcements. When a wide variety of information is shared, employees will feel more closely identified with the company and contribute more to its success. When everyone participates in solving a service problem, for example, higher-quality solutions will emerge from the greater input of ideas than would be the case if only a few managers know of and try to solve the problem. The rule to follow is to communicate as much as possible and, if need be, err in the direction of overcommunicating.

Communications should be a two-way street, as they are with the successful companies in our survey. They utilize an open-door policy and actively encourage employees to bring forward their concerns. Managers and supervisors deal with these concerns by showing empathy with the employee, listening intently, and trying to find a solution. Even if the outcome is not completely satisfying to employees, they know that they had a fair opportunity to express their feelings, be listened to, and be dealt with fairly. And that contributes to a climate and culture for success, one that is based on trust and openness.

While the day-to-day interactions between managers and employees determine much of the company's communication effectiveness, there are other activities that can be made a part of the culture, such as periodic open-forum meetings for employees, with a senior manager or skilled facilitator in charge. At such meetings, employees can discuss workplace issues and concerns and offer suggestions for improvement, which management can act on whenever it makes sense to do so.

One of the leading companies in our survey uses the "skip-level" meeting, a one-on-one session between an employee and the boss of the employee's boss. Employee job attitude surveys are another communications vehicle for identifying and acting upon issues and concerns. For surveys to be effective, management *must* provide candid feedback of results and take action on at least some of the identified problems. Activities such as surveys are good ones to be described in the culture statement.

Another important aspect of work climate is ethics and fairness. As with communications, management behavior here sets the tone for the company's operating style and should be addressed in the culture statement. For example, if a company's management tries to take advantage of clients, its employees will focus on using any means to get what they want from the company. If a company tries to circumvent certain laws and regulations, employees will do the same with company policies and procedures. The tone for internal employee actions is influenced very strongly by management practices with others.

What should be included in a company's statement of ethics? First of all, the company should express its desire to be responsible corporate citizens, conducting business in a law-abiding manner and maintaining a workplace that is safe and environmentally desirable for both employees and the community at large. Such ethics statements might also emphasize involvement in community and public service activities and donations to nonprofit community organizations.

Fairness and objectivity in dealing with both employees and outside organizations should also be emphasized in the company ethics statement. Fairness means that employee relations issues will be resolved objectively, without bias in regard to race, sex, or other personal factors, and that hiring and promotion decisions and performance evaluations will be based on objective, job-related factors. When such a tone is established, managers are likely to behave in accordance with it, and the company's image in the community will be enhanced. Employees of the human resources period will feel positively about companies that address such issues, since these are important matters for them.

Management Style. The ideal management style for the human resources period, the style that is most compatible with jobs and employees in the workplace of the future, is a participative, delegating style. The company's culture statement should include some definition of management style that is similar to this. Management characteristics that might be mentioned include the delegation of decision-making authority to the lowest possible level, encouragement of creativity, use of open-door practices, and an emphasis on change and improvement. Specific practices should be tailored to the needs of the individual company. The traits that are described in the culture statement will be translated into hiring and promotional criteria and the performance standards that managers will try to meet.

Company Policies and Practices. The culture of the industrial period was based on a multitude of policies, procedures, and work rules to govern the workplace. Some company policy manuals grew to the size of an unabridged dictionary, with policies to cover just about every conceivable event that could occur in the workplace. One modern-day industrial company has a large conference room filled with floor-to-ceiling files of policies, rules, grievance hearings, and arbitration cases. The cultural tone set by this is one of confrontation and a belief in going by the book.

The human resources period will see a reduction in the number of policies and rules that companies utilize. With jobs becoming more professional and white collar, there is less need to legislate work. Needless policies will get in the way of doing the job efficiently. Workplace freedom will be required for employees to do their jobs properly, and that means the absence of policies and rules. The leading companies in our survey had very slim policy books, and these were referred to as little as possible. As an outstanding example of this trend, Dana CEO Rene McPherson personally destroyed twenty-two inches of the company's policy manuals and replaced them with a one-page memo outlining Dana's commitment to employee development.

As an illustration of how needless policies get in the way of the workplace of today, consider one large company's policy on lunch hours. This policy states that everyone is entitled to one hour for lunch, and this lunch hour must be taken between 12:00 and 1:00 P.M. As a result, everyone goes to lunch at exactly 12:00 P.M., including senior managers, whose dining room serves lunch only during this time. How well does such a rigid policy lend itself to the work that needs to be done? Professional and managerial work does not end promptly at 12:00, so why should employees have to take a lunch hour at exactly that time? Would it not be more effective to take an earlier or later lunch hour to accommodate the needs of work flow? And what is true for professional and managerial employees is just as true for other employees, since the regimented jobs of the industrial period are a thing of the past.

To set up an effective culture, managers should continually ask themselves, "Do we really need a policy in this area?" If they cannot convince themselves that one is absolutely needed, then they should not have one. It is better to err in the direction of too few policies than too many. This way of thinking, exactly the opposite of that of the industrial period, is compatible with the work force and jobs of today. Employee productivity and satisfaction will be greater with more freedom from unnecessary workplace legislation. The company culture should emphasize this.

Case Study: Too Much Security?

The CEO of a high-tech company in Silicon Valley recently told me of a visit he had made to a new computer software firm in his area. The software firm, which had sprung up quite dramatically from very humble beginnings, had just leased a large new office building and hired a number of new employees. The chairman wanted to show off his new facilities and invited the CEO to take a look.

When the CEO arrived at about 5:30 P.M., as many employees were leaving, he immediately noticed the extremely tight security measures. Everyone had to pass through a gate in the lobby to enter any of the corridors. A uniformed security guard stationed at this gate would not let anyone enter without a badge. Visitors had to be met in the lobby by a representative of the company and had to sign in and wear a badge for the duration of the visit. Employees also had to sign in and out, even when going to lunch. Employees leaving the building had to open their briefcases or purses for inspection by the guard, apparently to ensure that nothing was removed without authorization. Security was equally tight throughout the rest of the building. The chairman explained that this security was necessary to ensure that no one stole the company's confidential software.

The next day the CEO said to me, ''What does all of that security tell a new employee of that company? It says, 'We don't trust you.' Furthermore, 'We expect you to steal from us,' and that is why all of the tight security abounds.'' He pointed out that if employees really wanted to steal from the company, they could conceal the software on their persons or copy it via phone modem to their computers at home. His feeling was that the company's behavior set a culture and tone that actually *encouraged* employees to steal.

Similarly, if a company has countless work policies and rules, the message to the employee is, ''We expect you to try to cheat the company or not work hard, so we have policies to cover every possibility. That way, we can be covered when we have to fire you.'' If the culture of a company indicates that employees cannot be trusted, they will behave accordingly. Establishing a culture and style that build trust and honesty will encourage these behaviors.

Hiring and Career Development. It is tempting for a company to say that it wants to hire only the best. However, that needs to be backed up with actual practices. Some companies that say that they hire the best may screen out candidates whose salary expectations are a few dollars above the suggested starting level. It is better to say what you actually practice. And do successful companies strive to hire the best? A total of 54 percent of the highly progressive companies in our survey hire only the best, whereas only 30 percent of the less progressive claim to do so. The more successful and profitable companies tend to look for high-quality employees.

Co. STATEMENT
Regarding
hiring

A company's culture statement regarding hiring practices could include alternatives to a statement that it hires the best. For example, it might state that the company hires only those who want a long-term career, or those who have excellent interpersonal skills, or those who are committed to high quality standards. Such culture statements become the informal selection standards against which job candidates are judged. The company will tend to hire only the employees whose characteristics match those expressed in the culture statement, so care must be taken in writing this part.

Related to hiring practices are opportunities for career development. Companies should promise only what they can deliver, but those progressive in human resources will have much to offer in the area of career development. For example, they might offer job rotation opportunities for long-term management development, extensive training courses, career guidance assistance, or college tuition assistance. The culture statement should describe what is available, since this is a high priority for many new employees.

TUITION
AIDE
Training
Career
Guidance

Another aspect of career development is the actual process of moving into new jobs. Progressive practices in this area include open posting of available jobs, promotion from within, and opportunities for movement into management positions by nonmanagers. This issue should be candidly addressed in the company's culture statement, since it is an important one for employees of the human resources period. Care must be taken not to oversell the promotion process, or too many employees will come to expect opportunities available to only a small percentage of the work force.

Posting
Promotions

Pay and Benefits Practices. Chapter Five contained a discussion of suggested compensation practices for the human resources period. Whichever of these practices a company uses should be included in its culture statement. For example, the statement might mention that the company is market driven in compensation, that it pays above the marketplace level, that it pays for performance, or that it offers flexible benefits for employees to select from. These and any other related practices should all be described in the culture statement.

Case Study: Prime Computer

Thus far our discussion of company culture has covered the types of components to include in the culture statement and suggested practices that are in tune with today's workplace. How does the human resources or line manager put all of these ideas together? What does the final culture statement look like? We present here the following highlights of Prime Computer's excellent culture statement entitled "Statement of Corporate Purpose" (n.d.). (Reproduced by permission of Prime Computer, Inc.)

- *We must provide products and services of outstanding value.* Prime must offer quality and value in its products and services. To maintain this focus, we must continue to keep customers' needs first and foremost in our minds.

   All Prime systems must be competitive on a price/performance basis. Further, our products and services must perform, reliably, as represented. We must never overstate our products' capabilities.

   We must continue to produce products of innovative design and technical excellence. We must provide service which is friendly, prompt, and a good value for the money. Good service is a customer's right, not a favor we bestow.
- *We are committed to creating an environment of personal growth and development.*

   Excellence in hiring. We strive to hire the best talent available at every level.
   Pay related to performance. It is our policy to pay for performance.
   Strong opportunity for growth. We believe that career development planning is a shared responsibility between managers and employees. The

goal is to help each individual realize his or her full potential.

Personal development.
Open communication.
Risk taking.
Adaptability.
Teamwork.
Personal health and safety.

- *We must produce exceptional profits.* Our ability to generate profits is the direct result of the way in which we manage our assets—our people, our facilities, our finances. Further, the ability to continue making profit at above industry averages is related to our ability to manage our assets better than others in our business.
- *We will grow to become a multibillion-dollar company.* Our goal has always been to grow at a faster rate than our industry, and we believe we will be able to continue to do so in the foreseeable future. Because of the company's policy of promoting from within, wherever possible, growth will mean increased opportunities for personal advancement and fulfillment.
- *We must be responsive corporate citizens.* Our policies include:

  Active support for affirmative action
  Active encouragement of employees who wish to pursue outside interests in public activities
  The maintenance of facilities which are a credit to the community
  Donations of corporate money, equipment, time, and services to worthy non-profit organizations
  Support and fair treatment of outside vendors
  The conduct of all our business in a fair, ethical, legal and responsible manner

- *We must maintain management excellence.* Prime's continued growth and success requires that our managers develop well-defined plans, exhibit good work habits, have the respect and confidence of subordinates, and be innovative and consistent in their decision making.

    It is our policy to encourage decision making at the lowest possible level. We feel strongly that this is the single most important way of avoiding the bureaucracy that frequently inhibits the growth of many medium-size and large companies.

    We don't manage by directive. It is the manager's responsibility to work with his or her people and use their ideas to improve strategies, techniques, and administrative systems.
- *We will control our own future.* Our company is different from others. It is different in our approach to the market. It is different in the extraordinary skill and teamwork of our employees. And it is different in the measure of success we've been able to share with both employees and investors.

This culture statement serves as a clear blueprint for managers and employees to follow in conducting their day-to-day activities. And it is an excellent way to sell what the company is all about to prospective new hires. Below we present ideas on how to communicate and reinforce such a culture statement.

Communicating and Implementing Company Culture

Most companies present their culture ideas in specially designed orientation programs that concentrate exclusively on the company culture. Such a program should not only describe the culture but also provide examples to demonstrate each key element and allow open discussion and questions. Many companies combine a culture program with presentations by senior managers and a thorough description of the company's products and services.

If the company culture is new or revised, all current employees should attend an orientation program that explains it, and the program should be presented to all new employees shortly after they join the company. Such a culture program could take a day or longer, particularly if a full explanation of the company's products is included. Are companies willing to invest this much time in culture and orientation? The Survey of Organizations found that 38 percent of the companies high in human resources progressiveness spent more than one day on orientation. Only 29 percent of the less progressive companies did so. Clearly, the progressive and financially successful companies spend more time on explaining the company to their new employees. Doing a thorough job of explaining the company is related to financial success.

There are other means of communicating the company culture besides formal orientation programs, including a variety of useful reminder systems. One of the leading companies in our survey has a plaque in the company lobby listing the key points in its culture. Another prints them on laminated three-by-five cards that are given out to everyone for easy reference. Still another lists them on poster-size wall charts that are hung in many individual employee offices and framed for display in the company corridors.

Most companies hold employees accountable for living up to the credo of the company culture. For example, if managers are to practice the open-door policy, then they are evaluated on this at performance appraisal time. Their final performance appraisal ratings, and ultimately their salary increases, are based in part on how well they perform against the company's culture. This is an excellent way to reinforce the ideas contained in the culture statement.

Another way to reinforce the company culture is through items in company newspapers or magazines. In addition to articles explaining the culture, they might include stories on how employees have lived up to it. For example, if prompt, courteous customer service is a part of the culture, then employees might be cited for good performance in this area, with specific examples of what they have done. Many company CEOs issue newsletters to employees in which they can cite examples of employee behavior in line with the culture or expand upon the key ideas in the culture.

Job candidates should know of the company culture before they join the firm. They should be given copies of the culture statement during the job interview to inform them of the type of environment the company provides and enable them to determine whether it is compatible with their personal beliefs. Doing this before hiring can save recruiting costs and make assimilation into the company much easier.

In summary, communicating the company culture must be more than a one-shot orientation program. There are many ways to get the message out and reinforce it on an ongoing basis. When this is done, the culture becomes a part of the inner fabric of the company, and people will practice the suggested behaviors and continually remind each other of the need to do so. Thus, a valuable employee need for affiliation can be fulfilled, and companies can better attain their goals.

Culture Change

Changing the company culture is an intensive process, but one that can be successfully carried out in even a relatively short period of time. At Heller Financial, which was discussed in Chapter Five, a massive cultural change occurred when the company was purchased by the Fuji Bank of Japan. Heller changed from a commercial lender making relatively small loans to one making large, upscale loans of as much as $75 million. From having fairly unprogressive human resources practices (for example, limited training and development, management that was not employee oriented), it became quite progressive in human resources, with state-of-the-art training and development and employee-oriented management. And much of this change occurred in a year's time.

In Heller Financial's case, the pace of change was accelerated by a new senior management team coming on board. But that is not necessary for culture change to occur, as long as the existing senior managers are supportive of building a new culture. Human resources managers should have a key role as catalysts in changing the company culture. They should sense when the timing is right for such a change—when the old way of doing things is not working as well as it could, when some managers are trying to initiate needed changes in the company's way of doing business.

How does a manager bring about a significant cultural change? First of all, bring together the senior management team and gauge their feelings about such a change. Without their support, the effort would be futile. If there is a desire to change the company culture or formally establish one where none existed, the head of human resources should take on the role of facilitator. With the culture elements presented earlier in this chapter as a guide, meetings should be held with senior managers to flesh out a culture statement such as that of Prime Computer. The culture statement can contain many areas beyond the components presented in this chapter, but they are a useful starting point.

The meetings with senior managers should focus on obtaining a consensus position for each culture idea. For areas where there is no consensus, a culture statement should not be developed, for the company's practices in such areas are not uniform. After initial drafts of the culture statement are developed with the senior managers, they should be circulated to a large number of employees for comment and then edited as needed. Once the final version is prepared, it should be communicated and implemented. While massive culture change is not easy, it can bring about a big payoff for the company, and it can endure.

Action Steps for the Human Resources or Line Manager

A number of actions can be taken by human resources managers or senior line managers to establish or modify the company culture; specific suggestions follow.

1. The first step is to determine whether any formal culture even exists at your company. Many companies have an informal culture but nothing very formalized or specific. Determine your current situation by talking to mid-level and lower-level employees. Ask them questions such as:

- How would you describe the mission of our company?
- How are we different as a company from our competitors?
- What are the company's key goals for the next couple of years?
- What type of management style does our company have?

If answers to these questions are vague or unknown, you need to strengthen the culture. Even if senior managers clearly can answer these questions, the culture is not filtering down to the lower levels.

2. The next step is to get the support of the senior management team. Go to them with the results of your survey and suggest that the culture be more formally established. Sell the positive benefit—that if employees better understand the company mission and goals, they can work more effectively. The results of our survey suggest that highly successful companies work toward building a clearly defined culture.

3. Assuming that the senior management team supports such an effort, begin developing the culture statement as described above.

4. The key to a successful company culture is to have more than a one-shot program. Spend time developing the mechanisms for making your culture a long-term success, such as orientation programs, company newsletters, letters from the CEO, posters, plaques, laminated cards, videotapes, recruiting materials, and performance appraisal forms that tie in with the culture. The informal culture should also support your efforts. Try to get managers to talk about the culture in staff meetings and one-on-one interactions with employees, with statements such as ''That's not our company's way of handling it. Remember, we strive for a high-quality product.'' ''In addition to the experience and education you are looking for in that new

manager, remember to look for a management style that is compatible with our culture.''

Summary

The human resources period has been given that label because people, human resources, are now essential for success. This is so because of the growth of the service sector and professional jobs and the substantial investment that companies make in hiring and training employees. In many cases, people are the only product. In recognition of the importance of human resources, successful companies will build a strong culture based on people. Elements that might be addressed in the company culture are the company mission and goals, communications, ethics, policies, work climate, management style, hiring, development, and pay practices.

Human resources or senior line managers are the catalysts to get a formal culture statement developed. Once it is put together, there should be thorough communication to employees and ongoing support programs to ensure that the culture is long-lasting and effective. Dramatic changes in culture are possible if the senior management team is committed to them. Successful companies examined in our survey make vigorous efforts to build and support a culture that strongly emphasizes human resources. These efforts are reflected in greater financial success for these companies.

7

Designing New Jobs
and Redesigning Old Ones

The Changing Job Market

The greatest job growth during the human resources period has been in white-collar and service occupations. White-collar jobs, which include managerial, professional, and office positions, made up only 18 percent of all jobs in 1900; today the figure is 53 percent. Add to this the 14 percent of all jobs that are service-oriented, and the total for white-collar and service is now over 67 percent. This number will continue to grow as the service sector grows and more professional and technical jobs are needed to support the new technology.

The increase in white-collar and service jobs is paralleled by the decline of other jobs because of automation. The U.S. Office of Technology Assessment (1984) recently found that the fewer the tasks involved in a job, the more likely it is that the job will be taken over by computer-assisted manufacturing. Simple, routine, repetitive jobs are most likely to be taken over by a machine. Occupations that would suffer the most are low-skill labor jobs, clerical support staff, craft workers, and lower-level supervision in these areas. On the manufacturing side, many assembly-line jobs will go by the wayside, as will those of welders, solderers, punch-press operators, lathe operators, machinists, and general laborers.

On the office side, file clerks will disappear as more and more filing is electronic computer filing, done by professional staff. Typists and low-level secretaries will be replaced by professionals and managers who "type" their own memos and reports on personal computers. This trend will really explode when voice-activated word processing takes hold. Many mail clerks will be replaced by robots that sort and deliver mail, and even the robots will give way to electronic mail.

Telephone operators have largely been replaced by machines already. You can call anywhere in the world without the assistance of an operator, make credit card calls without human assistance, and even have computers talk to other computers without a human intervening. Directory assistance has become more automated and will continue to do so.

Many bank tellers have been replaced by automated teller machines that can be used for making deposits, withdrawals, and fund transfers. Gasoline can be purchased in many places by automated machine. Goods can be purchased through computer terminal or television set, and in many cases no human is involved. Machines are even taking over more complex diagnostic tasks that involve "thinking," such as telling you what is wrong with your car, your stomach, or your mind. Jobs have not been replaced here yet, but can that be far away? The elimination of more routine jobs because of automation is a concern for many in the workplace today.

Action Steps for the Human Resources or Line Manager

What should a human resources or line manager do about the elimination of jobs because of technology? Following are some suggestions.

1. Audit the jobs at your company by assessing the number of tasks people perform on each job. You can likely get this information from job descriptions or other similar sources. Rank order the jobs by task variety, with the jobs having the fewest tasks at the top of the list. Jobs with three or fewer tasks should be labeled as "vulnerable" to being replaced by automation. Delete from the "vulnerable" list those jobs that are very people-

intensive, even if they have few tasks (for example, employment interviewer). Add to the list any supervisors of the jobs remaining on the list. Recognize that the jobs on your "vulnerable" list will be the first to be replaced by technology.

2. Talk to the managers of the jobs on the "vulnerable" list. Ask them whether there are plans to more fully automate the area. Could this happen even if there are no current plans? If so, when? Will all such jobs be replaced, or only some of them?

3. Inventory the skills and abilities of those employees in jobs potentially affected by automation. Can the employees be placed elsewhere? Can they be trained to do other jobs at your company?

4. Put some plans into motion before the automation change hits in full force. Train people for other jobs and identify places where they might transfer. This can save you some valuable employees and outplacement costs. As anyone in human resources knows, the more time you have to deal with training and placing employees, the more likely it is that the outcome will be positive.

Case Study: Preparing a Business Memo

Perhaps one of the most common tasks in business, done millions of times each day, is preparing a memo or letter. It is a task that has changed dramatically in the past few years, altering the nature of many jobs. Consider first how the task would typically be done in the industrial period. The starting point would be for a manager to write the memo in longhand on paper. The longhand original would then be given to a secretary for typing on a typewriter. After the memo was typed, it would be forwarded to the manager for proofreading and changes. Corrections would be made with correction fluid or eraser. If the changes were significant, the entire memo would be retyped and the whole process started over again. Once the memo was in final form, it would then be copied by the secretary and sent to those on the distribution list. The manager and secretary would probably keep paper copies of the memo for their personal files. Those receiving the memo might make additional copies to circulate to others.

The entire process was very time-consuming and highly labor intensive. The memo had to be written, typed, proofread, corrected, retyped, copied, mailed, and perhaps recopied. That takes significant human resources, not to mention paper, ribbons, copier fluid, and envelopes. Other than writing the memo, the work involved was not very challenging. Typing, copying, retyping, addressing envelopes, and mailing are all repetitive tasks that offer very little in the way of learning or creativity. The manager's proofreading the final copy is also not very fulfilling.

Consider now how the task will be done in the human resources period. In the ideal situation, all employees, including managers, have computer terminals with word-processing capabilities. Managers still have to write the memo, but now they do it on their own computer terminals. This takes no more time than writing by hand, and maybe even less, since editing is easier on a word processor.

After writing the memo, the manager might send copies via electronic mail to all of those on the distribution list. This is done by merely pushing a few buttons. A copy of the memo can be kept on a computer file. Those receiving the memo can read it, discard it, or send it to others electronically. That is all that there is to the process.

This process is less labor intensive and uses much less time and money than the industrial-period version. Probably an hour or more is saved in doing something as simple as preparing a memo. And what has happened to the secretary in the human resources period? That job is entirely "out of the loop" in the production of the memo. The manager has actually "taken over" part of the secretary's job in the production of memos. Those managers who do not like this idea might note that it takes them no longer to write the memo by computer than by hand, and a really big savings is made, since secretaries or typists are no longer needed to type memos. The savings in salary, benefits, and staff overhead are substantial.

Those managers who do not like the idea of touching a keyboard, or regard it as "secretary work," are rapidly finding themselves out of date in the workplace. That computer terminal sitting on the desk not only enables the writing of memos but is an excellent tool for gaining access to information such as production updates, budget performance, and even the latest news. The failure to adopt this new technology is a costly mistake affecting the bottom line, just as it is inefficient to use any other procedures that are out of date. In summary, the use of new technology can result in the elimination of a routine, repetitive job, in this case that of a traditional secretary or typist. It is also important to note that the manager's job changed here as well, with the addition of a new task formerly done by another. The "new" secretary's job that results is different, too, and we discuss that difference in the remainder of this chapter.

More Meaningful Jobs

The white-collar and service jobs of the human resources period differ significantly from those jobs of the industrial period in the amount of meaningfulness they can provide. The jobs of this period, such as those of computer programmers, attorneys, accountants, consultants, auditors, engineers, technical sales and service staff, and technical support staff, are complex jobs that require more thinking, learning, analysis, and problem solving than the jobs of the industrial period. They also involve a great deal of information exchange.

Toffler (1980) estimates that people employed in such occupations spend approximately 80 percent of their time in some form of information exchange, such as writing or reading communications, attending meetings, or participating in telephone conversations. The vast majority of all occupations, not merely professional jobs, will eventually involve information exchange. Norman Feingold (1983), president of National Career and Counseling Services in Washington, D.C., estimates that 80 percent of workers employed by the year 2000 will probably be employed in the information industry.

And why are these white-collar, information-oriented jobs more meaningful? Such jobs inherently provide more challenge and cannot be performed through very circumscribed procedures. Consider the robot technician job of the human resources period. Here, the robot has replaced the assembly-line job but created the technician job. Someone merely servicing such robots must understand computers, complex machines, production techniques, product quality, and so on. That job is much more meaningful than the work of an assembly-line production worker. And that is the type of job that is created when the assembly-line jobs are eliminated.

The example presented earlier showed how a manager had "taken over" part of the secretary's job in preparing memos. And what does the secretary's job now involve? Rather than typing and filing, the secretary will probably perform a broad array of tasks that were formerly part of the manager's job—project assistance, the tracking of budgets, computer entry and retrieval of data, and many other assignments related to the department's operations. The boring, routine job has been replaced by a much more challenging job, requiring learning, creativity, and higher-level skills. The typical job, even in staff support, will be more meaningful than the job it replaced.

Some might argue that this human resources revolution is still not reaching the average employee, that such innovation will not affect their particular business, at least for many years. Such skeptics might be interested in some findings of the Public Agenda Foundation's comprehensive study of the workplace (Yankelovich and Immewahr, 1983). This study found that 44 percent of the work force have *already* experienced significant technological changes in their jobs in the past few years and that 74 percent of those who have experienced such change feel that it has made their jobs less routine and more challenging and interesting. The change has definitely occurred; the challenge is to allow it to reach its full potential.

Case Study: The New Steelworker

The steel industry has long been regarded as a traditional smokestack industry that is far removed from the new revolution in the workplace. Are traditional industries such as these affected by the workplace revolution? Are the new jobs replacing the old ones in steel as in other industries? Or is such activity limited to service or high-tech firms?

Inland Steel, headquartered in Chicago, is an interesting case study. Inland's history in steel making goes back nearly a hundred years. All of its production facilities are located at one enormous plant in East Chicago, Indiana. Inland makes a wide variety of steel products, with much of its business targeted toward the automobile industry.

Just like many other large organizations, Inland has long used major computer systems. They have been an important part of corporate staff support operations in finance, accounting, human resources, and other areas. The adoption of word-processing technology for clerical support began in the late 1970s and continued into the 1980s. Inland has an on-line computer system that is available for sales and customer service personnel. The system tracks production schedules and the exact status of all products. The sales or customer service representative can check on a customer's order or product inventory by merely hitting a few keys on a terminal.

Perhaps the best example of how new technology creates and eliminates jobs is related to Inland's $1 billion investment in new production facilities in the late 1970s and early 1980s. At the core of this investment was a new blast furnace for making steel. Traditional blast furnace operations are very labor intensive, requiring crews of a couple of hundred to make molten steel from raw materials. These traditional blast furnaces, of which Inland has a few, are not very technologically advanced.

Inland's new blast furnace has a number of high-tech bells and whistles. The heart of the blast furnace department is a control room nicknamed "Star Trek" because of its circular shape and large number of video monitors, computer terminals, and electronic gauges. Production is no longer controlled from the hot shop floor by people wearing hard hats but by technicians sitting in an air-conditioned room watching monitors. The technician can mix the raw materials and modify the steel-making process at any time by merely pushing buttons, watching the entire process on a video monitor.

This technology of the human resources period requires vastly fewer and different people than during the industrial period, even in a traditional industry such as steel. The new jobs are those of technicians, computer programmers, electronics experts, and people who understand the "big picture" in steel making—all very meaningful jobs. The old jobs that have been eliminated are those of general laborers, craftsmen, work crews, ladle operators, and their supervisors. On the office side, many of the clerks and typists are gone, replaced by higher-skilled assistants and professionals. In the steel industry as well as nearly every other industry, the workplace revolution has had a very dramatic impact by creating new, meaningful jobs and eliminating others.

Action Steps for the Human Resources or Line Manager

Following are suggestions as to how a manager can best handle these new more meaningful jobs.

1. The new jobs, by their very nature, are more meaningful and rich than those of the industrial period—so long as managers do not design away their potential or overmanage them. As an example, the new assistant (secretary) jobs should include significant project- and service-related tasks and little of the traditional typing and filing. You need to audit such jobs at your company to see if you are moving in this direction. If jobs are designed and managed for only the "typing and filing" routine, frustration will result. Successful companies in the Survey of Organizations built meaningful jobs into their organizations, and you need to do so as well.

2. There are a variety of jobs that should now be more meaningful. Examine your jobs on both the office and manufac-

turing sides for the level of responsibility they entail. Upgrade where necessary, and plan on eliminating the more routine jobs.

3. If your audit shows that the jobs at your company are not designed to realize their potential meaningfulness, redesign them and include the new responsibilities in the job descriptions. Coach and counsel individual managers so they can reassign appropriate parts of their jobs and upgrade jobs such as that of secretary. Build these ideas into your management and supervisory training programs.

4. The skills of your employees should also be examined. Maybe the reason that some "secretaries" have not become "assistants" (or assembly-line workers have not become computer repairers) is that they lack the necessary skills. After identifying such employees, think of training and upgrading to prepare them for bigger jobs. The failure to do so will mean losing employees who are unable to handle the new jobs and new technology when they are introduced. If you have significant numbers of employees in this category, plan to add more people with the requisite skills.

New Workplace Freedom

The new jobs of the human resources period offer potential for much freedom in the workplace—freedom to make decisions, to control the pace of work, and to implement one's own ideas. This is because the growing jobs of this period are white collar, and accountants, attorneys, consultants, and psychologists all need to have significant workplace freedom to properly do their jobs. This was the case in the past and will continue to be so in the future.

The same is true of the jobs that are changing dramatically in the human resources period. On the office side, the typist job of the industrial period offered little in the way of workplace freedom (how many ways can you type a letter?). There were few decisions to make, and those that had to be made were made by the boss. Ideas were not asked for, and it was easy to set up a structure and rules for just about everything. By contrast, the new job of assistant might involve working on projects, the department budget, and technical assistance with clients. Those activities should allow for much more workplace freedom if they are to be done properly.

On the manufacturing side, assembly-line jobs of the industrial period offered little workplace freedom, the workers being essentially human machines. But the new jobs of the human resources period, such as that of robot technician, offer a great deal of freedom. Such a position allows the employee to control the pace of the work, analyze problems, and make decisions. There is no "right way" to do the job, which requires making improvements in the production process and product quality.

Developing the Potential. In both the office and the manufacturing sides, the new jobs of the human resources period, even the lower-level jobs, are similar to white-collar professional jobs in terms of workplace freedom. This is not to say that every employee from here on out will have a high amount of workplace freedom; some, such as french-fry maker in a fast-food restaurant, will have little. But the *typical* job (engineer, consultant, technician) will have much potential for workplace freedom, certainly much more than the typical job of the industrial period.

That word *potential* must be emphasized very strongly. As with job meaningfulness, the potential for workplace freedom can be limited by overmanaging. Authoritarian managers who make all of the decisions for their employees, try to personally solve all of the problems that come up, are rigid about starting and quitting times, and constantly give direction instead of listening will thwart the workplace freedom that *should* exist with these new jobs. Many managers are still managing this way, since that is what they learned and inherited from the industrial period. But a new, different management style is required with these jobs (this new style is fully discussed in Chapter Ten).

Action Steps for the Human Resources or Line Manager

The following steps can be taken by a manager to ensure that the potential for workplace freedom is fully realized.

1. Audit your current company practices. Are employees at your company given significant workplace freedom? Is it as great as it could be? Pay particular attention to lower-level positions, since that is where overcontrol is likely to be greatest.

2. If workplace freedom is limited, try to increase it wherever you can. Where appropriate, build it into the formal job description. Coach and counsel with managers and train them not to overmanage. Encourage them to delegate more, to allow employees to set their own work schedules, make more decisions, and control their jobs more effectively. Set up an informal culture and style that support workplace freedom. Eliminate unnecessary department rules and regulations that thwart workplace freedom.

3. Set up an environment that allows employees to be treated as adults in responsible positions and gives them some authority and discretion. The highly successful companies in our survey did this because it results in greater individual productivity and better bottom-line results, as well as fitting the new jobs better and resulting in greater satisfaction for employees. Those are outcomes that every company should want.

Creative Generalists

Creativity will figure prominently in nearly all of the jobs of the human resources period. People in professional and managerial positions should have had significant opportunity for creativity for quite some time; the continued growth of these jobs will make this need even greater. Creativity will also be highly necessary in lower-level positions, such as those of assistant and robot technician.

Why is creativity needed so much? Very simply, the nature of the new jobs of the human resources period requires that employees solve problems and improve productivity. That means that creative solutions are needed, whether in assisting a client with a delivery problem or in deciding how to improve the current robots. Psychologists need to be creative in helping clients, and consultants need to be creative in assisting managers with business problems. In short, creativity should be a part of all of these jobs.

That *should* does not mean that creativity *is* a part of such jobs right now. Managers might reserve all of the creative elements for themselves and refuse to allow employee creativity. The record so far indicates that this is the case more often than not. Consider the movement into quality circles, participation teams, and the like in the late 1970s and early 1980s. Apparently, many managers felt that employee creativity was not being tapped to its full potential, or why would they need such programs?

Quality circles faded from the scene almost as quickly as they became a hot item, abandoned in many cases because of limited support from management. Managers might encourage creativity for an hour a week when the quality circle met, then behave as the same old autocrats for the rest of the week. Or they might simply not use the ideas that employees came up with, fearing a loss of power. The net result was that the circles did not accomplish anything of value for many companies and were seen as a waste of time by managers.

Of course, quality circles were the sizzle, not the steak. Managers were correct to recognize the need to tap the reservoir of employees' ideas; it is just that they went for a gimmick instead of a lasting solution. For companies and employees to profit from creative efforts, they need more than a once-a-week brainstorming session. The opportunity to be creative needs to be present in jobs *all* the time and receive support from management.

Do any companies do a good job at this right now? Consider Tandem Computers, one of the leaders in the Survey of Organizations. Jim Treybig, founder and president of the company, elaborated on creativity when he first put the company together, stating that it was a part of everyone's job to be creative and that employees must continually be searching for newer, better, and different ways to do things. This applied not just to computer hardware and software designers but to everyone who works for the company.

Employees at Tandem are told of this creativity requirement at the time of hire, and it is reinforced throughout their careers. Managers are told in training courses that they must not only tolerate creativity but actively *encourage* creativity.

Treybig says that management support for creativity is tested at times, since employees are bound to make some mistakes, but that is expected and is no reason to withdraw support for creative efforts.

Action Steps for the Human Resources or Line Manager

As a human resources or line manager, you have a role in seeing that employee creativity is actively encouraged. The following are suggestions on how to do this.

1. Assess the degree to which your organization encourages creativity. Is the authority for making creative improvements seen as the domain of managers and a few professionals, as in the industrial period, or is it a part of everyone's job, as it should be in the human resources period? If the former, you need to be the catalyst to see that it becomes a part of everyone's job.

2. One of the more difficult activities for managers is asking for their employees' help in providing a creative solution to a problem. Many managers feel that they were made managers in the first place because of their technical knowledge and ability to solve problems. They feel that to go to their employees for this help is giving up a part of the job, making them feel less important. What managers need to realize is that employees are often closer to the problem—and the solution—than they are. Giving the employee at least the opportunity to solve the problem builds commitment to the solution and may result in a better outcome, since more people are involved in generating ideas. If creativity is delegated, the manager can, in turn, spend more time on planning, human resources issues, and other activities that there is often too little time for.

3. To build this creative responsibility among all, you need to start by getting top-level support. Your CEO, like Treybig at Tandem Computers, needs to tell both managers and employees that creativity is a part of everyone's job. This needs to be reinforced in orientation programs, training courses, and even manager performance appraisals.

A final question regarding the new jobs of the human resources period is whether they will be more generalist or more specialist. As we discussed earlier, the industrial period was known for highly specialized manufacturing and office jobs. The future will see a movement toward jobs that are generalist, as jobs were for many years before the industrial revolution. Why generalists? Consider the two benchmark jobs that have been used as examples throughout this chapter.

The robot technician must understand computers, robots, production methods, and electronics and have a systems approach to manufacturing. An employee in such a job will need to do preventive maintenance, troubleshooting, repair, rebuilding of components, and probably some design work as well. That is a very broad job in comparison with that of the typical assembly-line worker.

The same holds true in the office. A secretary in the industrial period might type, file, copy, and answer phones. In comparison, an assistant of the human resources period might need to understand computers for data entry and word processing, handle problems with customers, be a capable project assistant for technical work, be able to use sophisticated communications devices such as electronic mail or video or facsimile transmitters, understand accounting and budgeting procedures, and be able to plan and organize materials. That is a much broader job than before and requires many different types of skills.

Case Study: From 1,500 to 40 Jobs

In the late 1970s, Blue Cross and Blue Shield of Illinois began to recognize that highly specialized jobs were not the way to go. The company had approximately 1,800 employees in clerical and administrative support positions. Nearly every one of these employees had a unique job title and job description, some 1,500 altogether. Even file clerks in adjacent departments had their own job descriptions, though they performed the same activities.

Mutual employee support was made difficult with every desk considered a unique job. Employees were using the "it's not my job" excuse to avoid tasks not included in their job descriptions. Employees felt that performing such tasks might mean that they were doing a higher-level job without the commensurate pay. The large number of job descriptions also created an administrative nightmare for the compensation department. There was always a need to revise or update some job description. When union negotiations took place, the large number of jobs to discuss seemed insurmountable.

For these reasons, the company decided to drastically reduce the number of job titles and job descriptions. Positions were grouped into a half dozen job "families" and a few job levels developed for each family. Job descriptions reflected much broader, more generalist roles than before. The net effect was to reduce the number of jobs from 1,500 to 40.

The results were very positive. Employees understood the broader roles and enjoyed having more variety. The "it's not my job" syndrome began to disappear. It was easier to move employees into new jobs and provide vacation coverage. Tremendous administrative burdens were removed from corporate staff groups. All in all, it was a very successful outcome that has been experienced by other companies as well.

The Survey of Organizations assessed the extent of movement toward generalist jobs. Companies high in human resources progressiveness (and high in sales and profit growth) were twice as likely as less progressive companies to feel that the typical job in their company was a generalist. Altogether, nearly half of the highly successful companies said that their typical job was *already* generalist. That is a large number considering the difficulty of having generalist jobs at a large corporate headquarters, for example. The highly successful companies were also much more likely than the less successful to note a movement toward generalists at their firms. Clearly, the survey detected a movement toward more generalist jobs, with the successful companies leading the way.

This movement toward generalist jobs should not be taken

to the extreme. If everyone were responsible for everything, there would be great confusion as to who should do what. What the generalist trend signifies is that there will be broader roles for everyone and the elimination of narrow specialties. Also, there will be a narrowing in the differences between jobs, as in the case of the manager taking over part of the assistant's job in preparing memos and the assistant taking over part of the manager's job in doing project work. The net effect will be a workplace with broader, more similar types of jobs. These will be more fulfilling jobs so long as this trend is encouraged and not suppressed by management.

Action Steps for the Human Resources or Line Manager

Here is what managers can do to encourage this movement toward generalized jobs:

1. Recognize the movement toward generalist jobs and assess the trend at your company. Are your jobs moving in a generalist direction? Moving toward more specialists? Remaining the same?

2. Successful companies feel that the generalist trend is the way to go. Through job design techniques, try to broaden the roles of current jobs. Combine jobs or create more overlap in responsibilities. If nothing else, this will give you better coverage when vacations or terminations occur and make it easier to promote or transfer employees. More importantly, it will be more satisfying for employees and result in greater productivity.

Summary

Jobs of the human resources period will be significantly different from those of the industrial period. White-collar positions will continue to grow in importance with the growth of the service sector. Lower-level jobs will no longer be routine or narrow in scope as they were in the industrial period. The new lower-level jobs being created are very similar to professional and managerial white-collar jobs. They require a greater array of skills and offer more complexity and diversity than jobs of the past.

The new jobs of the human resources period have the potential for great meaningfulness, much workplace freedom, creativity, and broad-based (generalist) activities. This potential, in order to be realized, must be carefully managed. A stifling, control-oriented management can eliminate all of the potential inherent in these jobs, resulting in employee dissatisfaction, reduced productivity, and possibly turnover. Unfortunately, it is just such a management style that has persisted at many companies to this day.

To reap the potential benefit of the new jobs, human resources and line managers need to start by evaluating their current jobs and management styles. Jobs should be designed to be meaningful and broad-based and to allow for a fair amount of employee decision making, creativity, and control. These expectations need to be communicated to employees and become a part of the company culture as well as the job description. Management training and performance appraisals should reinforce the creation of such jobs and a participative way of managing them. Our survey has shown that financially successful companies have developed such jobs and manage them appropriately. That is one reason why these companies are financially successful.

8

Adapting to Changes
in the Work Force

The need for an entirely different workplace was created by new technology and the growth of service organizations. Thus far in this book, we have focused on the "macro" aspects of that new workplace. We have examined how the entire organization can be ideally structured, how jobs should be designed, the movement of jobs into the home, and the new corporate culture required for today's workplace. With this chapter, we turn the focus to the "micro" level—individual employees. Today's employees are vastly different from their predecessors, and these employee differences require companies to make a large-scale adaption or become less successful.

In the first section of this chapter, we consider changes in employee demographics. Then we examine the impact of these changes on the workplace—how they have created a need for new types of company programs and services. We specifically consider the following:

- The different needs of a new work force
- New employment trends
- Revamped employee benefits programs
- The profile of the successful employee
- Hiring techniques for the future

Employee Demographic Changes

As we mentioned in Chapter Two, education levels of employees have increased greatly in the past few years. Members of today's work force are much more likely to have college degrees and to want to put that higher education to use. Many other employee demographic characteristics have changed as well. Here, we consider the aging of the work force, increased diversity of the work force, immigrants in the U.S. work force, and changes in households and marital status.

The Aging of the Work Force. When the baby boomers first entered the job market in the 1970s, the effect was to dramatically lower the median age of the work force. In 1970, the median age was thirty-eight, but by 1982 it had dropped to under thirty-five, according to the U.S. Bureau of Labor Statistics. Now, as the baby boomers grow older, and the entrance of newer workers slows, the median age is increasing again. The U.S. Bureau of Labor Statistics recently pointed out that we are about to experience the oldest work force in our recorded history. By 1995, the median age is expected to be over forty. The elimination of the mandatory retirement age will further cause a graying of the work force.

On the positive side, this trend means that employees of the future will be more experienced than their predecessors. That should lead to productivity gains, since experience often translates into better productivity, and organizations will thus find it easier to decentralize and staff more leanly. However, some of this productivity gain could be offset by the movement to more complex jobs that require a great deal of change and learning.

There is a negative side to this aging of the work force as well. Employees entering the work force now will find a large group of baby boomers ahead of them. Some of the baby boomers will be in management positions, and many others will be lined up for the next management vacancies. Younger employees will find it difficult to advance into management. Making things more difficult yet will be the "flattening" of the management hierarchy and elimination of levels of management. Human resources and line managers will be hard pressed to address the needs of those who want rapid promotions.

Case Study: Help Wanted (Desperate)

There is a "double whammy" waiting to strike in the United States that will cause a shortage of employees in certain geographical areas in the coming years: a declining birth rate and employee migration trends. Before discussing the impact of these two trends, we will review their sources, beginning with the declining birth rate.

After the big surge of baby boomers in this country, birth rates declined. According to Wattenberg (1987), there must be 2.1 births per woman during her childbearing years if a nation's population is to remain stable over a period of time. If fertility rates fall below 2.1, the population will eventually shrink. Since 1970, the fertility rate in the United States has been 1.8 births per woman. In Western Europe, it has been only 1.6 births, with West Germany at only 1.3 births. Wattenberg (1987) forecasts that by the middle of the next century, West Germany will have only half the population that it does today. The forecast is not much better for the United States—a population decline is predicted for this country as well.

This declining birth rate means there will be fewer employees available for the work force. This trend has already affected us to a great degree. In the 1970s, the work force grew at an annual rate of nearly 2.5 percent. The rate for the 1980s is only 1.3 percent, and it will slow even further in the 1990s. By the early twenty-first century, there will be no growth at all, with the available work force actually declining. More than 75 percent of the employees who will be working in the year 2000 are already adults, and most are currently working.

If the declining birth rate and fewer employees are not enough in themselves, consider the added impact of migration patterns (see Chapter Four). Migration will create short-term geographical winners and losers in the battle for employees, but in the long run everyone loses unless the birth rate swings dramatically upward. If the working-age population is considered to be those between twenty and sixty-five, then the Northeast has been experiencing a *decline* in available employees since 1980. This is due to both a declining birth rate and migration away from the Northeast. By the year 2000, there will be at least 500,000 fewer potential employees in the Northeast than in 1980. The North Central region will essentially break even between now and the year 2000.

The South and West regions will show a short-term surplus in those available for the work force. The work force in the South will have grown by 30 percent by the year 2000, for a net gain of perhaps twelve million employees. In the West, the work force will have grown by 40 percent, creating a net gain of approximately ten million employees. But even these gains will not last forever. Despite migration gains, the declining birth rate will eventually affect the South and West as well.

The declining availability of employees will hit particularly hard a labor-intensive company growing rapidly in the Northeast. Are there any developments that can reverse this trend? The birth rate itself shows no sign of reversing thus far. The tendency for people to remain single and start families later would suggest that the trend has not even bottomed out. Work at home might prevent some migration from the Northeast but will probably not be enough by itself to reverse the trend. Immigration (discussed later) will also help but will probably not provide the employee technical skills needed by companies. Competition for skilled employees will likely be fierce as time progresses.

A More Diverse Work Force. The workplace has been dominated for many years by white male employees. As recently as 1950, white males made up 62.5 percent of the work force, according to the U.S. Bureau of Labor Statistics (1984). But that figure has changed greatly in the past few years. In 1984, white males made up 49 percent of those in the work force, the first time in history that they were a "minority." This decline is a result of recent gains by women and minorities in the workplace.

Women now make up nearly 45 percent of the work force, and the percentage is likely to grow even more as options such as work at home, contract employment, and part-time employment increase. Alternatives such as these enable many women to manage both career and family responsibilities much more easily than in the past. The net result is a growing female presence in the work force.

Members of minority groups (including minority-group women) now constitute 15 percent of the work force. These numbers, too, are increasing each year as more minorities enter and gain a foothold in the workplace. The actual number of minority-group workers is even greater when you add those who are working in this country with a temporary permit or working here illegally. The total number of minority employees is significant and reflects the growing diversity of the work force. That work force is no longer made up largely of white males.

Immigrants in the U.S. Work Force. It is estimated that as many as one-fifth of all employees in this country are not U.S. citizens. These "guest" workers either are foreign nationals who hold temporary work permits or are working here illegally. While actual numbers of such people are difficult to estimate, most forecasters agree that the total is increasing. Recent changes in immigration policy served to "grandfather" many of these employees, even those working illegally, and make them eligible to become U.S. citizens. But that will not change the increasing dependence on guest workers in this country.

According to U.S. Bureau of the Census projections, 22 percent of the U.S. population growth between 1980 and 2000 will be a result of immigration. Employers will increasingly turn to this immigrant group to fill jobs since our declining birth rate will not produce enough employees to fill the void. But many immigrants will lack the communications or technical skills to fill many of these jobs. Employers will have to devote increasing time and effort to training in order to assimilate these people into the workplace. There simply may be no other choice.

Human resources and line managers need to plan for this event now.

Changes in Households and Marital Status. Household size in the United States has been declining steadily for a number of years. The typical household now has 2.6 people. While the declining birth rate has accounted for some of this drop, an even greater factor has been the growth of one-person households.

The number of people living alone began to grow in the 1950s and 1960s and then exploded in the 1970s ("Living Alone . . . ," 1987), when the number of men living alone increased by 97 percent and the number of women living alone increased by 55 percent. While the rate of increase slowed somewhat in the 1980s, the increase continues. Currently, 25 percent of all households are one-person households, and in major metropolitan areas, more than one-third of all households contain just one person.

While much of the increase in one-person households is the result of people living alone after the death of a spouse or a divorce, the tendency to remain unmarried longer has also been a factor. For example, in 1970, 55 percent of all males aged twenty to twenty-four were unmarried, according to the U.S. Bureau of the Census. By 1985, the figure had increased to 75 percent. The percentage of women aged twenty to twenty-four who were unmarried increased from 36 percent to 57 percent during the same period. Clearly, the trend has been to postpone marriage longer and to have fewer children.

Perhaps the most interesting statistic of all pertains to the disappearance of the typical family unit. Currently, over 75 percent of all households in this country do *not* have two spouses and children, once the typical family unit. That means that many of the employees in the workplace do not come from typical family units. This has many potential consequences for employers, as we discuss later in this chapter.

Action Steps for the Human Resources or Line Manager

Though no one can change employee demographics, there are activities that can be carried out at any company to understand current trends and prepare for the future. Specific suggestions follow.

1. Start by compiling a profile of the current work force at your company. Look not only at race and sex but age, education, marital status, and the number of "guest" workers who are foreign nationals. What are the figures for your company? How do they compare to the figures cited in this book and other sources? Your analysis will be particularly interesting if you can get comparable data from, say, five years ago or more. Is the average age increasing? Are education levels higher? Are there more single people now than before?

2. A plan should be put together to address the aging of the work force. Assume that the effects of the baby boom will limit promotional opportunities for younger new hires at your company. How will you handle this?

First of all, be candid with your new employees. Do not tell them they will typically become a manager in a given number of years, even if that was the trend in the past. It may be harder to deliver on these promises now, and false expectations lead to morale problems.

Second, look toward an alternative career path strategy that does not involve movement into management. For example, create an individual contributor career path for accountants and programmers that could result in several promotions without moving into management. Communicate this as an optional career track that employees can choose.

Third, rotating assignments every year or two will provide many of the staff with learning, growth, and satisfaction even if they are not moving vertically. This may also help qualify employees for a broader number of management jobs, so they have more potential for vertical advancement. Long-range incentive plans, as discussed in Chapter Five, will also help keep these employees.

3. The potential shortage of skilled employees in the Northeast and perhaps the North Central regions presents a difficult challenge. Work at home should be pursued aggressively, as it might save some employees from having to relocate outside these areas. The relocation of some or all of the company's opera-

tions is another way to "join them if you can't fight them." Several companies have recently moved their headquarters from Manhattan to other locations, among them J. C. Penney, which has moved to Dallas. A significant base of operations in the South or West will mean a larger supply of employees to tap. Recent immigrants present another option for dealing with employee shortages in the Northeast. If you pursue this option, extensive training will be needed to develop the communications and technical skills of these employees and help them be productive in the workplace.

The Different Needs of a New Work Force

The work force demographic changes just presented depict a vastly different "typical" employee. Employees now are more likely to be single, to be older, to be members of minority groups or women, to have a college degree, and to live alone. And in many cases the employee might be a second wage earner who does not want a full-time job. That is quite different from the typical employee of the industrial period, a married white male with a high school education who was the sole wage earner in a family that included two or three children.

In the past, it was easy for companies to tailor their employment practices for a relatively homogeneous employee population. Now, however, employees are much more diverse and have different needs and expectations. Companies need to be flexible in their view of the employment relationship to accommodate individual needs. They will need to give employees more autonomy and control over their lives in the workplace. The failure to do so could mean difficulty in attracting new employees or the loss of valuable employees to more flexible employers.

In the remainder of this chapter, we will examine the workplace with an eye toward accommodating these new employee demographics, specifically considering employment trends, benefits packages, and hiring techniques, three of the primary areas where changes need to be made. Human resources or line managers should consider surveying employees to determine how well the workplace is meeting employee needs. For example, is the new work force dissatisfied with a five-day, forty-hour work week? Would more flexible work schedules be preferable? Is the standard benefits package working, or would more flexible benefits be preferred? The answers to these and similar questions may be surprising to employers who have failed to consider the changing demography and needs of their employees.

New Employment Trends

The industrial period was characterized by rigidity with regard to employment relationships. The vast majority of employees worked full time and put in five eight-hour days each week, possibly with some overtime. Starting and quitting times were fixed, and even the lunch period was fixed at many companies. Such an employment relationship is still the most common, though it no longer fits the needs of many in the new work force. Here we consider some alternatives.

Part-Time Employment and Job Sharing. Many employees do not want or are not able to work a traditional full-time job. Women with children and older workers facing retirement frequently have to make an all-or-none choice regarding employment. For many, that choice is to leave the company. This means the loss of a valuable employee for the employer and the loss of additional income for the employee. A solution to this dilemma can be found through part-time employment or job sharing.

Part-time employment has been particularly attractive for women re-entering the work force after spending time as homemakers. Nearly one-third of the former homemakers entering the work force have chosen part-time over full-time work. Such work options give employees the opportunity to simultaneously pursue family and career options. Part-time employment has proved attractive for men as well. Besides permitting more time for family matters, part-time work has been useful for those who want to pursue education and work at the same time, those who want to work in two entirely different career areas simultaneously, and those who want to work on a limited basis after retirement.

Have financially successful companies expanded the use of part-time employment? Results of the Survey of Organizations showed that 54 percent of the highly progressive and financially successful companies reported a recent increase in the number of part-timers on the payroll. Only 30 percent of the less progressive companies noted a significant increase in the number of part-time employees. It must be remembered that many of the highly progressive companies already have a significant number of employees working part time and so may not have noticed an increase. Even without considering this, results suggested that the increased use of part-time employees is related to financial success.

Since the 1960s, the number of employees working part time has grown nearly three times as fast as the number working full time. According to the U.S. Department of Labor fourteen million people outside of agriculture, some 14 percent of the total work force, are voluntarily working part time. Another six million (6 percent of the total) work part time out of economic necessity. Forecasters are predicting that the voluntarily part-time group will grow to over 20 percent of the work force by the year 2000 and may eventually reach 50 percent of the work force.

Most voluntarily part-time employees are in service, trade, and white-collar industries, with large numbers working in banking and insurance. These are exactly the industries that are growing right now. Diane Rothberg, director of the Association of Part-time Professionals in McLean, Virginia, sees an increasing shift in part-time employment to jobs in management, consulting, and high-tech professions (Rothberg and Ensor, 1985). The temporary help industry, which has been doing very well, places roughly 20 percent of its 700,000 employees in professional and technical occupations.

Closely related to part-time employment is job sharing. Companies pioneering the job-sharing concept include Levi-Strauss, TRW, United Airlines, and New York Life Insurance. According to a recent survey by the American Society for Personnel Administration (1986), some 20.2 percent of all companies surveyed have positions with two or more employees sharing the same job. Though less common than part-time employment, this is yet another vehicle that employers should keep in mind in accommodating the needs of a diverse work force.

Flextime. The jobs of the human resources period are less dependent on the clock. For many positions, starting the work day
a bit earlier or later than one's peers has no appreciable effect
on job results. For some jobs, even doing the work in the middle
of the night is possible. The workplace of today is not dependent on the synchronized, assembly-line operations of the industrial period. Companies that cling to rigid starting and quitting times are doing so merely out of tradition or the desire to
control, not out of necessity.

Employers in tune with the human resources period will
build more flexibility into work hours. One option is flextime,
which gives employees some choice over their starting and quitting times, as long as they put in the required number of hours
each week. The extreme version of flextime would put no restrictions on when the hours are put in. However, most companies
require that the employee be present during a core period, say,
10:00 A.M. to 3:00 P.M., and allow employees to decide how
early they want to arrive or leave.

Flextime permits employees to avoid rush hours, schedule
child-care needs, and take care of personal business during conventional work hours. It better fits the needs of women with
family responsibilities and of singles who find it difficult to take
care of home and personal business during weekdays. The
growth of women and singles in the workplace suggests that flextime is a needed option for employers. Companies with such
an option are more likely to be able to attract and retain many
of today's prospective employees.

Are companies moving to flextime scheduling? A recent
survey by the American Society for Personnel Administration
(1986) found that a surprisingly high 49 percent of companies
used flextime. Our Survey of Organizations found that companies progressive in human resources and financially successful
were nearly three times as likely to use flextime as the less progressive firms. Allowing for flextime is associated with company
financial success. The leading firms practice it, and that is one
of the reasons they are more financially successful.

The Use of Contractors and Retirees. Another growing trend that
meets the needs of today's work force is to include the use of

contractors and retirees in place of regular employees. As contractors, individuals work for a company for a specified number of days or a specified project but are not considered regular employees. The use of retirees, as either contractors or regular, part-time employees, is another growing option being favored by both retirees and companies. What benefits are there to being a contractor? First, as with part-time employees, contractors are able to pursue family, educational, or dual-career interests while they work. Second, being a contractor provides a great deal of flexibility and independence as to when to work and whom to work for. Many employees today are attracted to this flexibility and independence. Third, contractors have a chance to work for a variety of employers and test out a number of skills without the consequences of accepting and perhaps quitting a permanent job.

The benefits to employers are also significant. With the rapid change in organizations today, what was once a predictable world now is very unpredictable. The need for certain employees may suddenly arise and then as suddenly disappear. Permanent staffing is costly and slow to implement. Contract staffing enables employers to increase or decrease staff quickly and inexpensively. Further, labor costs are much lower with contractors than with regular employees, largely through savings on benefit and overhead costs. Alan Ewalt, senior vice-president of human resources at National Medical Enterprises, where 10 percent of the staff is contracted, estimates a 25 percent savings (personal communication, March 1987). Others go as high as 50 percent. Many managers are now buying human resources from the outside just as they would buy raw materials. They contract out when the need arises, stop contracting when the need no longer exists, or bring in a different type of contractor when that is needed. No longer are internal, permanent personnel regarded as the only way to provide human resources services.

There is, of course, a negative side to the use of contractors. Contractors may need extensive training for certain types of jobs and may not approach their jobs in the way that the employer prefers. This is all the more reason for companies to have clearly defined culture, goals, and training programs. Such programs will help contractors to understand the company's expectations. This problem does not arise with retiree contractors, who already know the company and its products and services. Some combination of outside contractors and retirees would seem to be particularly effective.

A recent survey of nearly 500 companies by Commerce Clearing House (1987) found that 36 percent made use of contract employees and 32 percent made use of retirees. The airline industry has long made use of contractors. At USAir, the proportion of employees who are hired on contract has recently grown from 10 to 22 percent. General Electric has recently farmed out the processing of insurance claims that were formerly handled by in-house personnel. AT&T now has data-entry work done exclusively by outside contractors instead of the hundreds of in-house employees who performed it in the past. Contractors have enabled many companies to decrease staffing requirements while still increasing sales and meeting the needs of the new work force of today.

Case Study: Alternative Work in Practice

Merck is a large pharmaceutical company that finished in the top twenty in the Survey of Organizations. Like many companies in that group, Merck is a leader in experimenting with alternative employment. The company uses flextime at most of its facilities in the United States and employs a number of part-time workers, including employees sharing jobs and retirees working part-time. Women have outnumbered men in part-time capacities by nearly a three-to-one ratio. The part-timers have worked in a number of positions, including management, professional, and clerical staff.

Merck realized long ago that traditional full-time employment did not fit the needs of a changing work force. Working mothers, dual-career couples, and retirees were just a few of the groups that were looking for other employment options. The company feels that it has an obligation to assist such employees and voluntarily instituted its work alternatives to reduce the conflict between job and home life. Rather than hurting productivity, such options are seen as *enhancing* it. Merck is conducting research to determine the long-term effectiveness of its alternative employment options, and early results are positive. Our survey found exactly the same trend across a number of companies.

Another company that has utilized alternative employment options is Travelers Insurance. Travelers makes extensive use of retirees as either temporaries, part-timers, or job sharers. Retirees can work up to 960 hours per year and still receive their pensions. Several years ago, Travelers sponsored an "Unretirement Party," a job fair to build up a job bank of retirees to fill various positions. The benefits of using retirees, according to Travelers, are the retirees' familiarity with the company and the job and their limited need for training. These benefits represent a cost savings over the use of temporary agencies. In a recent year, more than 450 jobs were filled through the retiree job bank at Travelers.

The public accounting firm Coopers & Lybrand has made extensive use of part-time employees at its ninety-five offices. Unlike the situation at some companies, many of the part-timers at Coopers are professionals, principally in the accounting and tax areas. Coopers & Lybrand found that alternative employment was needed to accommodate women wanting to start families, employees wanting to obtain advanced degrees and still work, and retirees wanting to work on a reduced schedule. The company sees part-time employment as a mutually beneficial work relationship that fills a need for both the employee and the company—an effective way of doing business at this time. That is the attitude of the progressive companies in our survey.

Action Steps for the Human Resources or Line Manager

Human resources or line managers have a key role in setting up alternative employment arrangements. The following steps can help them to serve as effective catalysts in this area.

1. Start by surveying your current employee population. What is the interest in part-time employment? Would some like to work as contractors if the opportunity were available? If you have not had part-time or contract work available at your company, chances are you have lost some employees for exactly this reason. Survey your former employees who left in good standing and your retirees to see whether they have an interest in part-time or contract work. Those who respond positively could form a pool to be tapped later.

2. Determine areas where part-time work is most feasible. Departments to consider are those with fluctuating staffing needs. For example, the accounting and tax departments will be particularly busy when compiling the annual financial statement and filing taxes. The systems area may be particularly busy when converting to new hardware or implementing new software programs. While clerical positions are the safest ones to experiment with initially, professional and managerial positions should be considered as well.

3. Examine the company from a "big picture" standpoint and ask whether there are activities being done internally that could be farmed out to contractors. For example, could data entry be done on a contract basis? Some accounting work? Security or janitorial services? Computer programming work? For those areas that can be contracted out, think of using smaller, independent contractors such as your retirees rather than large consulting firms. Contracting out routine accounting work to a consulting firm might be more expensive than doing it yourself. Using retirees might be less expensive yet, particularly when you consider that benefits and office space costs will likely be saved.

4. Communicate part-time and contracting options to your current employees so that they can sign up for such assignments now, or at least be aware of the opportunity to do so at a later time. By not communicating thoroughly, you may lose some valuable employees who might otherwise be retained.

5. The company should develop a pool of names for use as part-timers or contractors. When the need arises, someone in human resources can compare the requirements of an assign-

ment with the characteristics of the people in the pool. Part-time or contract work can be set up as permanent (until further notice), for a specified number of days, or for a specified project. Pay rates will have to be determined separately for each assignment. Paying a daily rate equivalent to the salary midpoint for the job will still produce a great savings, since benefits and overhead costs are saved.

6. Flextime is another alternative that should be examined. This is a nice benefit to sell potential new hires and, more importantly, meets the needs of the work force. Rather than have a totally open system, most companies designate core hours when everyone must be present. You need to designate these hours at your company, and then allow employee flexibility in starting and quitting times around those core hours.

Revamped Employee Benefits Programs

Employee benefits packages assumed their present form as benefits were tailored to the typical employee of the industrial period, a married male with children who was the sole wage earner in the family. New benefits were added to the package with this typical employee in mind, although they were made available to *everyone* in the company, regardless of demographic characteristics and need. Since the majority of employees fit the profile of the typical employee, there was little concern about whether they were appropriate for women or singles. For example, the two biggest benefit add-ons of the industrial period were family health insurance and employee life insurance. Family health insurance was an attractive benefit in the past, since family members besides the employee had no easy means of obtaining such coverage. Though insurance was available through personal subscription, that could be costly or impossible to obtain. A family package offered by the employer was an attractive option. Similarly, employee life insurance had an important role for the industrial-period family. The sudden loss of the sole wage earner could have a catastrophic effect on the family. Life insurance provided through the company was an attractive benefit.

However, the typical employee today is different from the typical employee of the industrial period. As the review of employee demographics showed, the work force is very diverse and no longer has a typical set of characteristics. For this reason, the standard benefits package will not appeal to many employees. Single employees with no dependents may not care about family health insurance. Dual-career couples do not need the "double coverage" of family health insurance that is furnished by each spouse's employer. Life insurance may not have much meaning or importance to young, single employees without dependents.

It is difficult, if not impossible, for any single benefits package to appeal to every member of today's diverse work force. Some employees will find either insurance, pensions, or vacations less attractive than other benefits. The solution lies in a flexible benefits program that allows employees to pick the exact mix of benefits they desire. An employee might select, for example, an extra week's vacation in place of life insurance coverage or pick between other options of equal cost.

Flexible benefits programs were developed in the mid 1970s by firms such as American Can, TRW, and Educational Testing Services. The Employers' Council on Flexible Compensation, based in Washington, D.C., estimates that flexible benefits programs are now used by more than 500 companies in the United States (personal communication, Ken Feltman, executive director, June 1987). Is the use of such a program related to a company's financial success? The Survey of Organizations found that 24 percent of the more progressive, more profitable companies used a flexible benefits program. Only 6 percent of the less progressive, less profitable companies had such a program. The use of flexible benefits is still another way for companies to meet the needs of today's work force and run a successful business. Those who implement a flexible benefits program are more likely to be profitable than those who do not.

Flexible benefits programs have been successfully implemented at many companies. Advantages cited by some of the leading companies include:

1. Greater employee satisfaction from benefits tailored to meet personal needs
2. "More bang for the buck" in benefit expenditures
3. Greater employee appreciation of the total cost of benefits when the trade-offs between benefit options are apparent

Problems have arisen only when companies offer too many options, causing an administrative burden. This has been controlled by limiting the number of alternatives for employee selection.

Case Study: Flexible Benefits at American Can

American Can pioneered the use of flexible benefits in 1978. The company offers employees "flexible credits" to use to purchase various benefits options, including medical insurance (six levels to choose from), life insurance, disability insurance, vacations, a retirement plan, a 401K plan, coverage of the costs of child care and adoption, and financial planning. Employees can spend their credits as they see fit and are allowed to periodically alter their coverage options. The benefits director at American Can found that the program is less expensive than a fixed benefits program, contrary to most people's expectations. Satisfaction with such a program has run high, generating about 50 percent more positive responses than received from employees at companies with traditional benefits packages.

Trends over several years showed that most employees were unlikely to opt for the most comprehensive medical insurance, instead choosing a plan that reimbursed a smaller percentage of expenses and spending the remaining credits for other benefits. This suggests that the very comprehensive medical coverage most companies provide may be replaced by plans with higher deductibles or less reimbursement of expenses if other benefits options are provided.

Action Steps for the Human Resources or Line Manager

Activities that can be undertaken to establish a flexible benefits plan are as follows:

1. Determine which benefits could most effectively be made flexible. For these benefits, determine what you now spend per employee as a fixed cost. You should now be able to determine a cost ratio between existing benefits.

2. Where possible, develop levels for certain benefits and determine the cost for each level. For example, medical insurance might provide for 80 percent, 90 percent, or 100 percent reimbursement of covered expenses. These levels are the choices that employees might pick from in spending their credits. Inexpensive benefits, such as travel insurance, should be left intact, since creating levels here would make the choices too complex. For a benefit such as medical insurance, there should not be a ''zero option''—all employees should have some coverage. Even those in perfect health could be financially devastated by an accident that runs up large hospital bills. This could also leave the company in a difficult position. With a benefit such as medical insurance, the only choices should be in deductible amounts or percentage of expenses reimbursed.

3. Determine what number of credits each employee will be given to spend. Put together a matrix chart with the ''costs,'' in credits, for each level of each benefit. For example, travel insurance might cost one credit, 80 percent medical insurance five credits, 90 percent medical insurance six credits, and so on. The value of a credit across benefits should roughly approximate its cost to the company. Your computer system will need to be configured to track employee choices. Planning this early is necessary, as is modifying your benefit plan booklets. Also decide on the frequency with which employees may change options. An orientation program to announce the new program is essential.

Profile of the Successful Employee

In earlier chapters, we have discussed the new technology, new jobs, and new workplace of the human resources period;

in this chapter, we have reviewed the demographic changes in the new work force. Considering all of these, what type of employee characteristics will be needed in the future? What sorts of skills, abilities, and traits are important for the new jobs and the new workplace? What would you need to look for as a hiring manager? The following are suggested traits and characteristics to look for in nonmanagement employees.

Being a Self-Starter. Work at home or at a small office park will involve limited contact with a supervisor. Flexible work hours will mean that employees start and finish work at their own initiative. Strong self-starters will be needed in this type of environment.

Ability to Work Independently Under General Supervision. White-collar and service occupations offer more independent work than industrial-period jobs. Since the new jobs of the human resources period are white collar and service in nature, employees will need to be more independent, and function well under less scrutiny, than employees of the past.

Ability to Adapt to Rapid Change. Jobs, companies, and technologies are changing more rapidly than ever before. This will require employees who are flexible, able to change direction, and open-minded about the dynamic workplace.

Mental Rather than Physical Abilities. Physical requirements will be minimal for jobs of the human resources period. Certainly, communications skills and manual dexterity will be very important, but even here, machines may assist the handicapped in performing these tasks. An alert and competent mind with analytical skills will be much more important than physical skills.

Ability to Learn Quickly. The rapid change mentioned earlier will also require employees to learn new jobs and tasks more frequently than ever before. The ability to profit from training and self-study will be essential.

Planning and Organizing Ability. Planning and organizing were done by the manager in the industrial period. Now, more of this activity has shifted to individual employees. Those who can anticipate workplace problems and opportunities and plan their activities accordingly will be more successful than those who cannot.

Creativity. The unstructured jobs of the human resources period will require a great deal of creativity from nearly everyone. Those who can analyze, innovate, and improve will be more successful than those who cannot.

It is interesting to note that these skills and traits are nearly the same set that employees needed prior to the industrial revolution. The only exception is physical abilities, which were more important then than now. Members of the new work force will need to acquire skills that are only partially developed by many people and not developed at all by others. With the proper training, employees should be able to master them, since our predecessors did so for many years prior to the industrial revolution.

At this point, managers should review their current work force in light of these skills and traits. Are the current employees strong in these areas? Are these characteristics looked for when hiring or promotion decisions are made? Specific techniques for evaluating such traits when hiring are presented in the next section.

Hiring Techniques for the Future

The jobs of the industrial period allowed for relatively simple hiring techniques. With relatively few skills and traits to select for, it did not take a great deal of effort or talent to identify good candidates for a vacancy. Take, for example, the job of typist. In hiring for such a job, an interview would be used to assess the quality of work experience and the "fit" between the employee and the company. Employment application forms would be used to screen candidates and check references. And a test, in this case a typing test, might be used to assess competence with the key skill. All in all, if done properly, this was a relatively quick and accurate process for making a hiring decision.

However, jobs of the human resources period are much more complex and involve a broader array of skills. What sort of test is there for measuring creativity or determining whether someone is a self-starter? The techniques of the industrial period are inadequate for evaluating these types of traits and skills. In deciding what will be needed in the future, first consider what techniques from the past can be carried over. The application form and reference check will likely remain unchanged and will continue to be used for screening and verifying employment history. The traditional interview can also continue to be used for assessing job knowledge and technical ability. Paper-and-pencil tests might still be used for assessing technical skills, though these tests are difficult and costly to develop for complex jobs. What else is needed?

Simulations, role plays, and assessment centers are techniques for assessing the more complex skills and traits. These are all variations on a common theme. A simulation is an exercise that replicates a part of the job someone is being hired for. For example, sales job candidates might be asked to give an impromptu sales presentation by which employers could evaluate presentation skills. Simulations provide the candidates with the needed background information to complete the exercise and do not require the person to be familiar with the company or its products.

A role play is a hypothetical situation that might be presented to a candidate in a job interview to assess traits that are difficult to evaluate with traditional questions about background and experience. For example, say you were interviewing candidates for a manager's job and you wanted to evaluate their ability to do performance coaching. You might introduce a brief role play in the interview, giving the candidate information about a hypothetical employee and manager, the performance problem, and other needed background information. You would then ask, "How would you handle this performance coaching session? What would you say or do?" Answers would give you insight into the person's ability to do performance coaching.

An assessment center is a collection of exercises that candidates complete over a period of time, perhaps two days. The assessment center can include simulations and role plays wherever appropriate. Assessment activity might also include exercises that test certain technical skills, such as scheduling abilities. The candidate would be given the necessary background information and then asked to schedule the work activities for a hypothetical staff. Given the number of exercises and the amount of time required for an assessment center, it is typically used for internal development and promotion rather than the assessment of outside job candidates. However, the technique can definitely be used for outside selection as well.

Leading companies have been using innovative selection techniques such as simulations, role plays, and assessment centers since the late 1960s. Early pioneers of these techniques included AT&T, IBM, and Standard Oil of Ohio. They have also been used by Sears, Olin, Cummins Engine, General Electric, J. C. Penney, Ford, and Merrill Lynch. By applying this new technology, companies can better evaluate the complex skills needed for human resources period jobs. That leads to more accurate selection decisions, better employees, and better financial results.

Case Study: Hiring a Compensation Manager

To illustrate the new hiring techniques just described, we consider their application in selecting a compensation manager. Traditional interview questions and reference checks have been used to determine the candidate's experience and technical job knowledge. However, to make a good selection decision, it is still necessary to evaluate the candidate's traits and skills in the areas of creativity, participative management style, delegating ability, and employee relations. How can these skills and traits be assessed?

Simulation questions could be asked in a job interview to assess the candidate's creativity. (Ideally, the same or similar questions would be asked of all job candidates.) Such questions might include:

- If you had to design a job evaluation system from scratch, how would you do it?

- Describe as many employee incentives that a company might utilize as you can think of.
- If you had to develop an ideal compensation philosophy for a company, what sort of ideas would you put into it?

Next, participative management style and delegating ability might be assessed through an "in-basket" exercise. This exercise begins with asking the job candidate to pretend that he or she holds a hypothetical management position within the company. The candidate is provided with background information about the position and staff. Also provided are a number of items that would typically be found in an in-basket. These range from irate letters from customers to general reports or memos from the boss. All the items require action, and the candidate must make written notes on how he or she would handle each item without discussing the alternatives with others.

After the candidate completes the in-basket exercise, an evaluator can determine how accurate he or she was in delegating items to the right people. Also, ability to use a participative management style can be inferred from whether the candidate kept most of the items for him- or herself (nonparticipative) or delegated wherever possible (participative).

Finally, employee relations skills might be assessed by a role-play question, such as "Say one of your employees walked into your office right now to raise a complaint. It seems that one of her co-workers is smoking too much, and this is bothering her so much that she cannot do her job. She is emotionally upset and wants action taken. What would you say or do?" The candidate would literally walk through his or her responses to this role-play scenario. Answers would indicate the candidate's skill and sensitivity at handling employee relations matters.

Action Steps for the Human Resources or Line Manager

Human resources managers in particular need to be in the lead in setting up selection techniques for the company. If your company is not using or is underutilizing more progressive techniques, the following can be done:

1. Simulations, role plays, and assessment centers could be used as part of selection procedures for every job in the company. The focus should initially be on the high-volume, benchmark jobs and later broadened to include other jobs. Fortunately, jobs can be grouped together for the purpose of developing hiring techniques. Simulations and role plays should be pursued first, since they are inexpensive and easy to develop. An assessment center can be added later if desired.

2. For each job, develop a list of traits and skills that are important to assess and cannot be determined through traditional interview questions. For each of these traits or skills, design a simulation or role play to assess skills in the area. The assistance of a skilled human resources consultant may be needed here.

3. Training will need to be provided to line managers if they are to be involved in using the simulations and role plays. An easier alternative is to have only someone in human resources do this part of the process.

4. When making the final selection decision, ensure that all of the relevant information is shared and discussed. Make comparisons between candidates on each of the skills and traits and combine this with the information on experience and job knowledge to determine who should be hired.

Summary

The new work force of the human resources period is substantially different from the work force of the past and presents new challenges for the human resources and line manager. Employees today are better educated than their predecessors, older than ever before, and more likely to be female, members of minority groups, recent immigrants, single, or living alone. Promotional opportunities will be difficult for many new employees, since there are a large number of baby boomers lined up ahead of them. This is a problem that human resources and line managers will have to cope with, as they will with the anticipated shortages of employees in the Northeast and other areas as a result of both a lower birth rate and migration away from certain areas.

The changing demographics of the new work force also suggest that our employee benefits packages need to be revamped. Benefits packages have historically been tailored for the typical employee, a married male with children who is the sole wage earner for his family. Given the diversity of the work force today, no single package will appeal to everyone. The solution is flexible benefits packages that permit employees to choose their own mix of benefits.

Finally, the skills and traits required for the new non-management employees cannot be assessed through traditional interviews and paper-and-pencil tests. The solutions developed by leading companies involve the use of job simulations, role plays, and assessment centers to make hiring decisions. Findings cited throughout this chapter show that companies employing such progressive human resources practices are more financially successful than those who fail to do so.

9

Strengthening
Human Resources Development

Employee development is another of the "micro" issues that companies need to address in the human resources period. Individual employees will need and demand more training and development in order to properly carry out their jobs. The rapid pace of change and the increasing complexity of jobs will require an almost nonstop developmental effort by employers. Companies that fail to properly train their work force will be less productive than their competitors.

Many companies have already recognized the need for increased training and development. *Training* magazine's annual survey ("Industry Report 1986," 1986) found that $29 billion was spent on formal training by companies in the most recent year. It was estimated that some 36.5 million employees in the United States received at least one hour of formal, company-sponsored training during that year and the total time devoted to instruction amounted to some 1.3 billion employee hours. The survey also found that middle managers were the most likely to receive training and clerical employees the least likely.

Employee development efforts can help companies achieve several important objectives. Programs in this area can:

1. *Build technical skills.* Rapid changes in technology and job content create the potential for employees becoming out of

date in their specialty areas. Companies need to assist employees in keeping up with the current knowledge in their field, whether it is manufacturing technology, finance principles, or computer skills.

2. *Develop more generalists.* As we noted earlier, there is a movement toward broader, more generalist roles in the workplace. Companies will need to help employees prepare for such jobs through training courses, job rotation, cross training, and other activities.

3. *Instill company culture.* Jobs are now more independent from one another than they were in the past. Employees may even be physically removed from a common workplace. Contracting is replacing full-time employment. These trends require companies to strongly communicate to employees the company culture, purpose, and mission.

4. *Foster creativity and innovation.* Creative, innovative efforts are needed by all employees if a company is to be successful. These skills will have to be developed for the many employees whose jobs did not include them in the past.

5. *Develop key employee skills and traits.* Building new skills and traits such as planning, independence, and flexibility in coping with change will require different, innovative approaches to training.

Basic Training and Development

In this section, we discuss the types of essential and basic development activities that all companies should regularly engage in. Basic training courses build broad skills that are needed for a variety of positions. Employers have an obligation to provide this training and update it as needed. The only other option, and *not* the recommended one, is to replace the staff every few years to bring in the requisite skills. That is a very costly alternative, and it does not enable a firm to maintain employees with significant knowledge of the company and its operations. Leading companies provide basic training and development in the following areas:

- Technical training
- Computer literacy
- Basic business knowledge
- Management skills
- Communications skills

Technical Training. Keeping up to date with developments in one's field will be a major need of nearly all employees of the human resources period. Accountants will need to be familiar with the latest accounting regulations, finance professionals with the latest financial methods and laws, and robot technicians with the latest equipment and servicing methods. Employees will increasingly come to fear being out of date in times of rapidly changing technology, as we are experiencing now. Companies that provide formal courses to upgrade technical skills will be able to attract and retain outstanding employees. The investment in training will pay off in better productivity and less turnover.

There are a variety of ways for companies to provide technical training. What is important is that there be some formal way for employees to acquire the knowledge and skills other than "learning by doing the job." The most common way to provide technical training is through classroom education led by an instructor who is an expert in the area, with a predetermined course of instruction. Another method, which is increasingly popular, is computer-based learning. Companies such as Control Data pioneered this method, which enables participants to go through the materials at whatever pace they choose. Quick learners rapidly move on to more complex material once they have mastered the basic material, as indicated by built-in tests.

Outside sources of continuing training for employees, such as seminars, workshops, and professional associations, enable companies to avoid "reinventing the wheel" with in-house courses. However, outside programs by themselves are not likely to provide the full array of needed technical training. A recent survey (Zemke, 1987) found that nearly 70 percent of all companies provided technical training but only 10 percent relied exclusively upon outside seminars and workshops.

Are financially successful companies more likely to have employees attend outside programs? The Survey of Organizations found that 76 percent of the progressive companies have their employees attend one or more out-of-town programs per year, while only 40 percent of the less progressive companies do so. Since human resources progressiveness correlates with financial results, there is a relationship between outside development of employees and financial success. Firms that are successful send their employees to more programs than do the less successful.

Professional credentials are likely to become more common in the human resources period. This has already become common for professions such as attorney, accountant, broker, auditor, nurse, psychologist, and physician. Other white-collar and service occupations, such as human resources professional and computer specialist, are moving in this direction. Company support and encouragement of employees seeking credentials will be needed as more professions require them and employees desire them to demonstrate competence in their field. The main forms of support requested by employees will be employer payment of credential fees and time off for exams.

How well are companies doing overall at providing technical education? A total of 74 percent of the highly progressive and highly profitable companies examined in the Survey of Organizations felt that they were doing a good job at technical education. Only 48 percent of the less progressive, less profitable companies felt that they were doing a good job here. Building a technically competent work force is related to a company's financial success. Those who spend the time and effort to build technical skills see a payoff in financial results.

Computer Literacy. The increased computerization of the workplace will require that nearly everyone have some basic competence in using computers. Whether their jobs require only an occasional look-up of information or nearly all-day data entry, everyone needs training in at least the fundamentals. There may be some reluctance on the part of senior managers to touch anything with a keyboard on it, but once exposed to the broad array of information available, they should become regular users, particularly when voice-activated word processing arrives.

While companies are fortunate that many schools are providing basic computer literacy training, they still need to provide training on how to use the company's unique computer system and all of the related software. Currently, 53 percent of all companies provide some sort of in-house computer literacy training ("Industry Report 1986," 1986). That figure will likely increase as more and more employees use computers in carrying out their jobs.

Basic Business Knowledge. As we mentioned earlier, part of a strong company culture is employee identification with company goals and objectives. However, before employees can identify with and support the company's goals, they must have an understanding of what the goals mean. For example, such goals might include targeted profit margins or return on equity, yet many employees may not understand these terms and be unable to follow the company's progress in attaining its goals. If managers decide not to communicate these goals at all, the result will be a gulf between managers and employees and less teamwork and mutual support in work activity. Training on the basics of business is a solution.

While colleges can certainly provide a good deal of education in this area, the company has an important role as well. Formal training classes can instruct on basic business principles and discuss them in light of the company's unique practices and results. Human resources and line managers can also encourage all supervisory employees to explain many of these ideas informally in staff meetings and through other vehicles. The net result will be an employee work force that understands and works toward attaining key company goals.

Management Skills. Management and supervisory training is the most common type of training offered by business organizations. Almost 77 percent of all companies provide some sort of management and supervisory training ("Industry Report 1986,"

1986). The wide range of important management skills that can be developed through training includes skills in planning, organizing, delegating, performance coaching and appraisal, goal setting, and many others. In addition, companies can provide training on the management traits and behavioral style that fit the human resources period. (What these traits are and how to provide instruction in them are discussed later in this chapter and in Chapter Ten.)

The leading companies in our survey use a practical, pragmatic approach to management and supervisory training, rather than a theory-based approach. They focus on practicing the skills in the course itself, so that the skills are easily transferred back to the job. How much management training do companies provide? Of the companies rated high in human resources progressiveness in our survey, 60 percent provided six or more days of in-house management training for managers. Of those low in human resources progressiveness, a mere 12 percent provided six or more days of in-house management development. Since the progressive companies were more financially successful, the results bear out the identified trend: investing more in management development results in better financial results.

Communications Skills. Communications skills have always been important in the workplace but will be even more important in the future, with the white-collar and service orientation of many jobs requiring interactions with others. Communications and interpersonal skills will need to be well developed for service organizations to be successful.

Communications skills training is further necessitated by the increased movement of immigrants into the workplace. For many, English is a second language. Even though education levels in the United States are rising, there is still a significant percentage of the domestic population with communications deficiencies. Companies will need to devote increased time to communications training to ensure that recent immigrants and other employees can fully carry out their jobs. Nearly two-thirds of all companies currently provide training in this area, and that figure is likely to increase.

Case Study: Training at Motorola

Training and development have been a part of Motorola's success for a long time. In the 1960s, the company began a series of executive development programs to complement its other offerings. In 1980, CEO Robert Galvin asked that a five-year plan for training be established. A task force made up of representatives from manufacturing, sales, engineering, and marketing helped assemble a plan. One of their recommendations was the establishment of the $11 million Motorola Training and Education Center, which opened in 1986.

The Motorola Training and Education Center runs three shifts a day and provides training for employees from entry-level manufacturing to senior executives. Each of Motorola's major business groups must budget at least 1.5 percent of its payroll for training. Actual expenditures have averaged 2.2 percent of payroll in the past few years. Motorola estimates that its 90,000 employees receive three million days of training per year, for an average of twenty-eight hours per year for each salaried employee.

Motorola's latest training course catalogue is 122 pages long. Roughly three-fourths of the programs are technical in nature. The catalogue not only describes each course and its intended audience but also includes the business issues that the course addresses. Among the courses listed are:

Advanced Electronics Microprocessors
Advanced Sales Call Dimensions
Applied Diagnostic Tools
Asset Management
Basic Electronics
Basic Statistics
Business Requirements Planning
Cause and Effect Problem Analysis
Competitive Awareness

Senior management support for training and development is one of the reasons why Motorola has had so much success. Both Galvin and chief operating officer (COO) William Weisz are part of the instructional team for the Competitive Awareness course. The two also serve on the advisory board of the Training and Education Center. Weisz says that he and the other managers set the proper example by attending the training courses themselves. They also monitor the performance of the business units in the company to see who is using the training and how effective it is. Motorola's attitude regarding training is very much in tune with the human resources period.

Action Steps for the Human Resources or Line Manager

Providing basic training is the minimum commitment that companies should make toward developing human resources. To ensure that such training takes place at your company, the following actions can be taken:

1. Start by assessing your current offerings. Are there in-house or outside courses available for technical education, computer skills, basic business, and management and communications skills? How many hours per year do employees spend in training? Do all employees participate, or just managers and technical professionals?

2. Gain senior management support for training. This is most easily done by assessing managers' training needs and then obtaining the budgetary resources to develop courses that meet those needs. Managers will see training as a good investment if the programs are results oriented and practical and help them attain their business goals. There is a training-related need for almost every business goal. Increasing sales might mean improving the sales skills of the existing sales force or hiring and training additional sales representatives. Introducing a new product requires training employees to sell, service, and support that product. Human resources and line managers should constantly

be on the lookout for training activities that could help the company attain its business goals.

3. The training and development function should be operated by highly skilled professionals. There is more to designing a training course than meets the eye. For example, training employees to make a good sales presentation is more than just explaining this to them, orally or in writing. The skills should be demonstrated, preferably by videotape. Key steps for making sales presentations should be developed for easy transfer back to the job. Most importantly, employees should have an opportunity to practice the skills and receive feedback and coaching. It takes a skilled professional to put all of these materials together.

The focus in training courses should be on building skills that are easily used back on the job, quite different from merely providing information about a subject, as is often done in college courses. But figuring out *how* to build these skills, through lecture, written material, skill practices, and other vehicles, is often quite complex. Professionals in the area need to be familiar with adult learning and course design—a former salesperson who is "good with people" may not be effective in this role. Human resources and line managers should ensure that the right people are leading the training function and resist the temptation to have mere content experts put together and run training classes.

Career Development

In the industrial period, the concept of career development was not very meaningful. Jobs were easy to learn and required few skills. Employees found themselves locked into narrow specialty areas with no skills to transfer to other areas. Promotions, where they existed at all, were usually hierarchical, such as from assembler to senior assembler or secretary to senior secretary. As a result of this, employees focused on the *job* rather than on a *career*. Attention was riveted on the end products of having a job—security, pay, and benefits. Boring, repetitive work was tolerated for the pay and benefits it provided.

As mentioned earlier, employees of the human resources

period are more interested in careers than in jobs. This larger concept of career goes beyond any given job or company. Career development is seen as a long-term process that includes ongoing self-assessment, education, training, on-the-job experience, and movement into new positions. The desire for career development has extended to all jobs within a company, even unionized entry-level jobs. Glenn Watts, former president of the Communications Workers of America, sees the twenty-first century as a period when "career-minded workers will insist on portable skills that they can take from job to job, regardless of the employer" (Watts, 1983, p. 83). Companies must address this career development need or suffer the consequences.

What kinds of approaches have companies used to address career development? One of the earlier career development methods was based on historical job movement trends. A company might analyze typical job movements over a period of years and construct job paths on the basis of the results. It might find, for example, that entry-level accountants typically became senior accountants two years after hire, then became assistant controllers two years after that. After these paths were mapped, they could be discussed with prospective or current employees in career development meetings.

An advantage of this type of career development program was that it gave employees the "big picture" of where they might be several years down the road. That could help with career planning, training, and eventual movement into other jobs. The disadvantages are that (1) employees might not want careers that follow the typical ladder but might prefer instead to move into jobs very different from their present ones; (2) those who are mismatched in their present jobs would find it difficult to find another career path; and (3) the typical career path is seen as too slow and traditional for the "superstars" of today, who are likely to want rapid job rotation, cross training, and quick movement to attain their career goals.

Another early method for addressing career development was the career planning workshop. Companies following this approach would sponsor an open-enrollment workshop for all interested employees. The workshop would typically involve a self-assessment of job interests and abilities and construction of a career plan for attaining personal goals. The advantage of the workshop approach was the opportunity it provided participants to develop greater self-understanding and to learn how to plan their careers. Disadvantages were that the workshop fell short of matching employees with specific jobs in the company—the process was a broad overview rather than focused and specific.

Progressive companies of the human resources period are using an integrated, systems approach to career development. Several key elements are critical to this integrated approach. First, it should include self-assessment. Employees need to understand their strengths, weaknesses, skills, abilities, and interests. It cannot be assumed that a particular person with a systems analyst job has the same strengths, skills, and interests as other systems analysts. He or she may have an entirely different profile, which suggests movement into other kinds of jobs down the road. The self-assessment should be "scorable" in the sense that results can be matched up with specific jobs in the company.

Second, jobs in the company should be grouped together for career movement purposes. While historical trends are a good starting point, the grouping need not be based on prior trends and can cut across departmental or functional lines. Job groupings should be based on similarities in ability and skill requirements, with all jobs in the same group requiring similar skills and abilities. The employee self-assessment should allow for matching to these specific job groups. In this way, employees can identify specific jobs in the company that match their unique interests and abilities. There are several techniques for developing this matching process. One of the most effective was developed by Johns Hopkins University professor John Holland (1973). Though Holland's work was intended for vocational guidance of students, others have extended it into business and industry.

Third, after grouping jobs, the company should compile information on the typical skills, experience, and education required for each job. In this way, employees can determine what they need to do to eventually attain a given job, and plan accordingly.

Finally, the company should have an open-minded perspective on career development and provide needed resources for the process, including sharing of information, career planning assistance, open posting of jobs, and allowing for job moves that might be vertical, horizontal, or diagonal. Managers should support the "loss" of a good employee to another department when it helps the employee attain a personal career goal and saves a valuable resource for the company.

Are companies providing career development assistance? Responses to the Survey of Organizations showed that 66 percent of the highly progressive and profitable firms offered some sort of internal career development program for their employees, while only 30 percent of the less progressive and less profitable firms did so. Once again, results confirmed a relationship between being progressive in human resources and financial results. The use of career development programs is associated with financial success.

Case Study: Career Development at Coca-Cola

Coca-Cola U.S.A. operates a fully integrated career development program that has tied together a number of elements that are kept separate in many companies, such as performance appraisal review, career discussions, and succession planning. The company's first activity in this area was training all managers in performance evaluation. Coca-Cola's performance appraisal process allows for each employee to be evaluated as to the attainment of specific objectives as well as other performance factors. Performance appraisal discussions often lead to career development discussions, which managers were trained to conduct one year after the performance appraisal training.

These career development discussions are regarded as two-way conversations focusing on employee growth, and not necessarily advancement. Employees at Coca-Cola are told that they are responsible for managing their careers, but managers have a key role in providing feedback about career interests and options. After the career development discussions, the managers complete forms summarizing the employees' career history, job interests, strengths, and developmental needs. These forms are then sent to the next level of management and then to human resources for review.

The last element of the process to be implemented by Coca-Cola was succession planning. The company holds "People Days," when each employee's readiness for the next level of assignment is reviewed by at least two levels of management. Individual development needs are reviewed and plans for assistance developed. The succession planning process includes an open discussion of moves across departments wherever appropriate to fulfill individual and organizational needs.

Coca-Cola makes a number of resources available to assist with career development. Job vacancies are posted, and job profiles are available to provide employees with information about specific jobs. A career planning workbook assists in assessing strengths and interests, and the company holds a two-day "Career Strategies Workshop" as well as a number of in-house training courses. These courses are described in a catalogue that lists the specific skills developed in each course. The company also offers a 100 percent tuition reimbursement program.

When vacancies occur at Coca-Cola, human resources managers review all sources of information to determine whether a match exists. Those sources include performance appraisals, career development discussions, succession planning reviews, and applications submitted. In this way, the system is integrated and ensures full consideration for all employees. The career development program at Coca-Cola is very much in keeping with the needs of employees and organizations in the human resources period. It is an effective way to assist individual employees and run a successful business.

Action Steps for the Human Resources or Line Manager

Human resources and line managers need to ensure that their companies have effective career development programs.

Specific steps to implement such a program include the following:

1. Have a fully integrated process for career development rather than merely a career workshop or suggested career paths. The integrated system should include self-assessment, a job grouping process, and some system for matching specific employees to specific jobs.

2. Develop a bank of job information that employees can tap. This bank might include job descriptions, job experience and education requirements, skills needed, and frequency of availability. Progressive companies are putting this information on software so that it is easily accessible and updated.

3. Provide support mechanisms to help employees attain their career goals. Such support mechanisms include tuition reimbursement, in-house training courses, career planning guides, and the open posting of job vacancies.

Nontraditional Training

Nontraditional training is training that goes beyond merely building skills or technical job knowledge. An example of this is providing training on company culture. The outcome here is not a new skill but an awareness of how the company operates and how each employee contributes to company success. A course in company culture should be at the top of every company's list of nontraditional training activities. Other areas that might be addressed in nontraditional training include:

* Productivity improvement
* Individual development
* Team building
* Personal health
* Management style
* Retirement planning

Productivity Improvement. One of the dilemmas faced by employees in a rapid-paced environment is how to pull back from the immediate job task and ask, "How can we make things better?" A nontraditional training course on productivity improvement can provide a formal means to address this question. Ideally, employees would be allowed to address any workplace issue of concern to them in a productivity improvement program.

An example of productivity improvement efforts is found at General Motors, which several years ago pioneered "participation teams." These teams meet regularly to discuss an open agenda of workplace issues, though the focus is often on production and quality. GM provides the teams with training in areas such as problem identification, brainstorming techniques, creativity, testing of solutions, and implementation of a final solution. Developing these skills enables employees to more effectively consider and resolve various productivity issues. Teams develop a resolution of workplace problems, present their recommendations to management, and hopefully receive approval to implement their suggestions.

Focus groups are another form of nontraditional training utilized by the successful organizations in our survey. These groups are formed to investigate and resolve workplace issues identified in employee job attitude surveys. The groups continue to meet until all issues are resolved. As with participation teams, skill development could be included in the activities of the focus groups.

Individual Development. Individual development programs are designed to create customized development plans for targeted employees. In the most common form of this type of program among the leading companies in our survey, a consultant first conducts an in-depth assessment interview with the targeted employee, usually a manager. The consultant then meets with the manager's subordinates, peers, and superior and asks them for confidential comments on the manager's strengths, weaknesses, skills, traits, and style.

The information from all of the meetings is combined with the consultant's own evaluation to compile a final report. The report presents a suggested individual development plan for the manager to follow. This plan includes on-the-job activities, seminars, readings, and other activities to help the manager improve where needed. The results of an individual development program are usually kept confidential, with the manager alone determining whether anyone else sees the report. The consultant becomes the manager's coach and counselor, whose only function is to help the manager meet the goals for improvement.

Closely related to individual development programs is the use of mentoring. An internal mentor, usually a senior manager, can serve in much the same capacity as the consultant in individual development programs. The mentor can provide advice, guidance, and counseling to an individual employee without the constraints that would arise if the employee's own superior played this role. Mentoring has been used extensively by companies such as Merrill Lynch, Federal Express, the Jewel companies, and even government agencies, such as the General Accounting Office. IBM, General Electric, ITT, Procter & Gamble, GM, and Ford have used mentoring to produce CEOs not only for their own companies but for other firms as well. Either mentors or individual development programs will greatly aid the development of employees, as the leading companies have discovered.

Team Building. Leading companies conduct team building for both proactive and reactive reasons. On the proactive side, team building is used to build mutual understanding of job roles, shared goals, and the individual traits of team members. With a skilled facilitator, periodic team-building sessions can ensure that individuals work as a cohesive group and support each other. They are particularly useful after a reorganization or the introduction of new employees into a department.

"Assimilations" are another form of proactive team building, used by companies such as General Electric to ease the transition when a new manager joins the company. In a typical assimilation, the new manager's employees meet as a group with a facilitator, outside the presence of the new manager. The employees brainstorm a list of questions and concerns about the new manager. For example, they might want to know about the manager's background or be concerned about possible changes in policies or staffing. Following the meeting, the new manager privately reviews the list with the facilitator and then responds to the employees' questions and concerns in a group get-acquainted session that can be followed up with individual meetings.

Physically demanding group challenges are still another form of team building. The idea behind these ventures is that away-from-work physical tasks, such as climbing a mountain or traversing a stream, will force company participants to help each other out. With the aid of a skilled facilitator, participants learn how such helping activity can be applied to the job. A more effective work team is the result.

On the reactive side, team building can be used to resolve problems when employees are not working together as a group. For example, if there are turf problems over who is in charge of an area, or two departments' employees do not get along with one another, a skilled facilitator will bring these employees together as a group and get all of the issues out in the open. Mutually agreed-upon solutions will then be worked out so that the employees work more as a team.

Team building is an effective means of developing cohesive work groups. While some would not regard team building as "training" in the purest sense of the word, it is nevertheless a form of employee development that increases productivity. Many teams acquire new skills and insights as they go through the team-building process and are then able to apply these skills back on the job. Leading companies find team building an effective means to run a successful organization.

Personal Health. Many employers, recognizing that a healthy work force is a more productive work force, offer nontraditional training in such areas as exercise, diet, nutrition, and psychological health. Companies point to the bottom-line payoff of such activities in terms of reduced absenteeism and fewer health-related benefits claims among the participants.

One of the foremost companies in health training is privately owned S. C. Johnson and Sons (Johnson's Wax). Johnson built a large fitness facility with exercise equipment, jogging paths, and park areas for the exclusive use of its employees. The company has a full-time health staff and sponsors classes in everything from aerobics to proper dieting and nutrition. They believe that it is an obligation of employers to provide for the physical health of employees.

Other health-related training sponsored by the leading companies includes health fairs and clinics. Screening is periodically offered for health-related problems such as high cholesterol levels and high blood pressure. Those who screen positive are given coaching on how to minimize their problem. Many companies have also sponsored training in areas such as quitting smoking. Employer involvement in employee health education can improve not only health but job satisfaction as well. *Training* magazine ("Industry Report 1986," 1986) found that 40 percent of U.S. firms have discovered this by offering health training to their employees.

Management Style. Much of the management training discussed earlier focuses on building *skills,* such as delegating or conducting performance appraisal reviews. However, some companies have discovered that there is a "missing piece" in management training, and that piece is training in management style. Managers not only need to possess management skills but also need to understand the most effective management style for utilizing these skills. Some companies provide this type of training as part of their culture programs or management skills courses. Others have stand-alone modules on management style or include it in individual development sessions.

One example of this type of training is a program to develop a participative management style. Training managers to be participative is more than just building skills in delegating. Such training also needs to cover how and when to practice participative management and how participative managers behave on the job. Similarly, building a people-oriented management style is more than communications and interpersonal skills training. Management style training might include how to practice the open-door philosophy or "management by wandering around," as advocated by Peters and Waterman (1982).

Management style training gets at the less concrete, less easily defined part of being a good manager. Obviously, the suggested management style will vary from company to company. What is right is what is desired by the particular firm. What is important is that there be some training on what a given company expects of its managers—how they should behave and act to be in concert with the company's practices and culture. Such training is particularly important for younger, newer managers.

Retirement Planning. Leading companies have come to recognize that the transition into retirement is a difficult one for many employees, especially those who lack an opportunity for part-time employment after retiring. A different financial situation and the loss of frequent contact with co-workers can be sources of stress. Nontraditional training in this area can help upcoming retirees plan for the future more proactively.

Training in retirement planning can cover a wide variety of areas. The most frequent focus is helping the employee ease into a different employment status. Training here might address, for example, how to start a new career through consulting or hobbies, which is increasingly common for retirees now. It might also discuss whether part-time or contractual employment should be accepted, should the employer offer these.

Another common focus of retirement planning is financial planning, with information provided on choosing investments, budgeting, adjusting to a new income level, and tax regulations pertaining to retiree income and Social Security. Such training will help former employees make sound financial decisions in the years after leaving full-time employment.

Retirement planning also may include advice regarding the adjustment to a different life-style and the absence of a network of co-workers. Psychologists might help retirees think through the trade-offs of relocation to another area and ways to maintain friendships after leaving the company. These and other types of retirement planning are being used by the progressive companies in our Survey of Organizations. Altogether, some 17 percent of companies offer nontraditional training in this area ("Industry Report 1986," 1986).

Action Steps for Human Resources or Line Managers

Human resources managers in particular should examine the potential for nontraditional training at their companies. At most firms, fulfilling training needs will require going beyond the traditional types of training detailed earlier in this chapter. The nontraditional training discussed here is being used by many leading organizations, but the specific programs any company uses will be based on individual needs. Human resources managers should use the six areas detailed in this section as merely a starting point in determining what their companies need. Since the development of nontraditional training programs requires different and creative approaches, the use of an outside consultant will likely prove helpful.

Summary

This chapter has discussed one of the most rapidly growing areas of the human resources period, employee training and development. Employees today want and need a great deal of development assistance to accomplish their career goals and remain technically proficient. The rapidly changing workplace requires frequent training for employees to carry out their jobs and ensure company success. Basic training is the minimal commitment that employers should make to their employees. Basic training includes areas such as technical skill building, management training, computer literacy training, building basic business knowledge, and developing communications skills.

Career development programs are also needed, since many employees today shun the traditional career path and want a career rather than a job. To ensure success, career development programs should be integrated systems that allow for self-assessment, the grouping of jobs into career families, and a matching of individual employees with individual jobs. We also recommend that companies provide career assistance such as tuition reimbursement, open posting, and in-house training.

The growing area of nontraditional training includes activities such as individual development programs, productivity improvement training, and team building. The progressive and financially successful companies in our Survey of Organizations are more likely to make extensive use of training and development than their less successful counterparts. These companies see development as a smart investment in human assets. With better training of the work force, employees are better able to do their jobs, which in turn leads to greater productivity and company success.

10

New Ways of Managing: Changing Roles, Relationships, and Styles in the Workplace

The human resources revolution has brought about a number of significant changes in the workplace. There have been changes in workplace technology, the nature of jobs, the place of work, company culture, organizational structure, and employee demographics. However, none of these changes can be successfully implemented unless there is change as well in one other area—management style. The traditional type of management, with its emphasis on control and authority, will prevent the successful implementation of the ideas presented so far in this book. What is needed is a new, different management style, a style that is in concert with the human resources period.

In this chapter, we consider the new role that managers need to take on in the future. Human resources and line managers need to personally assume this new role and ensure that others in their companies do so as well. Their personal involvement in the process cannot be overemphasized, for the changes in the workplace offer tremendous potential for both companies and employees. Our survey has shown many times over how progressive practices can turn that potential into better sales and profit results. Leaders who manage in tune with the new workplace can attain spectacular results. Ineffective leaders utilizing outdated practices can easily thwart the company's potential for financial gains. We discuss in this chapter five key aspects of the new management style:

- A movement toward general supervision
- Participative management style
- Fostering creativity
- Enhancing communications
- Staff selection and development

General Supervision

The industrial period was characterized by very close supervision. There was a mechanical, "right way" to do the job, with no deviation from the rules. Supervisors policed the workplace to make sure everyone was working and doing the job the correct way. Policies and regulations abounded, and supervisors spent much of their day ensuring compliance. Creativity and change were under the control of the supervisors, not individual employees. The overall supervisory style was tight, controlling, stifling, and highly circumscribed.

That same style persists to this day in a number of companies, since many current supervisors were mentored by those of the industrial period. While most supervisors today are savvy enough to avoid being obvious dictators or autocrats, subtle aspects of that style are still quite persistent. For example, a supervisor who becomes aware of a production problem might work out a solution independently instead of tapping the ideas of the staff, or even *thinking* of tapping their ideas. That is a less obvious way of being controlling and stifling staff creativity, but it is still very common in the workplace today.

Several factors have combined to render ineffective the controlling, autocratic style of the past. The first of these is the movement toward generalist white-collar and service-oriented jobs. These types of jobs are highly complex, with no right or wrong ways of performing them. They cannot be reduced to a set of steps or mechanical procedures. Therefore, a supervisory style that is tight and highly vigilant does not fit. The new jobs *require* a less controlling management style.

The changing nature of organizations has also made tight supervision obsolete. Fewer levels of management and more employees reporting to a single supervisor make it impossible for supervisors to be involved in every detail and decision. A controlling style of management would only serve to bottleneck operations and frustrate staffs. Clearly, the industrial-period way of managing does not fit this new type of organization.

The movement of work into the home also affects supervision. It is difficult, if not impossible, to closely supervise employees who are scattered at their respective homes, perhaps miles apart. More important, it is not *desirable* to closely supervise work-at-home jobs. Employees who work out of their homes will probably work different hours and have to be independent self-starters to function in such a capacity. Once again, close supervision does not fit with this type of employee or workplace trend.

If a tight, controlling supervisory style will not be effective in the future, then how should control be managed? We suggest that managers provide only general supervision during the human resources period. This general supervision is free of tight controls and close scrutiny, allowing for freedom and independence in carrying out the job, with only general reviews taking place. Managers should be more like coaches, counselors, and facilitators than tight, decision-making controllers.

Managers of the human resources period should use a minimum of workplace rules and regulations. For example, rigid starting times and lunch hours do not fit today's jobs and work force. Workplace rules should be done away with as much as possible, replaced by discretion and flexibility in handling individual employees. Similarly, thick policy manuals and "contracts" are no way to manage from here on out. Managers who "manage by the book" and rely on corporate policy will be out of tune with the work force. Instead, there should be a focus on doing what is right for the individual through the use of flexible, creative solutions.

General supervision will be made easier if the job roles of employees are broadened. Many white-collar positions already include a fairly broad set of responsibilities. The challenge here is for managers to ensure that they are not overmanaging these jobs by the use of many controls. The greatest opportunity for broadening is with clerical and manufacturing positions, with secretaries becoming assistants and assembly-line workers becoming technicians. However, a tightly controlling manager can keep a secretary a secretary, with the role restricted to typing, filing, answering phones, and the like. What the manager *should* do is proactively broaden the role to that of an assistant, involving computer work, project assistance, and other activities that are more complex in nature. This role is appropriate to the human resources period and fits with a general supervisory style. The same can be done on the manufacturing side.

The general supervisory role also relies on teamwork. Supervisors in the new organizations will typically supervise a number of employees. Rather than trying to manage all of the work group's activities, the supervisor of the human resources period should build self-management through teamwork. Members of the team can coach each other, provide feedback, and help with minor technical problems. The supervisor can also take on these roles, and will be able to do so more effectively when some of the burden is shared by the work team. Supervisors must proactively build teamwork, since it will not necessarily occur by itself. It is an important function to implement in using general supervision.

Participative Management Style

The industrial period was generally characterized by an autocratic management style. Managers were to make decisions on their own, solve all problems, strongly control the work of subordinates, and issue frequent orders on what to do and how to do it. The work of subordinates was felt to be less important than that of managers. When activities were delegated, it was the *task* (for example, compiling information) that was delegated; rarely was the *authority* (for example, to resolve a problem with a client) delegated. That management style is still more prominent today than most people realize.

Several factors in the human resources period require a

more participative style of management. The nature of the new jobs is the first factor. In Chapter Seven, we mentioned that the jobs of the human resources period have potential for more meaningfulness and workplace freedom. The tasks to be performed by a systems analyst, attorney, assistant, or robot technician are challenging, complex, and meaningful. Delegated responsibility, authority, and some decision making are necessary for these tasks to be properly carried out. However, all of this potential can be quashed by an autocratic manager who thwarts this potential job meaningfulness and workplace freedom. A participative management style is much more compatible with these new types of jobs.

A second factor driving the need for participative management is the decentralizing of the workplace. In Chapter Five, we mentioned the trend for companies to decentralize their operations and put in place smaller, local facilities. These local facilities are ideally run by managers who have a fair amount of autonomy and authority. An autocratic, centralized decision-making style would likely frustrate local clients, who would take their business elsewhere. A participative management style, which permits a fair amount of decentralized authority, would be much more effective.

A last factor fueling participative management is the new work force itself. In earlier chapters, we presented a profile of the new employee, an educated person who wants learning, challenge, and authority in the job. This new employee might be prevented from moving into management because of baby boomer effects. Unless "intrapreneuring" is used to fulfill promotional needs within the company, these new employees will leave to fulfill their needs elsewhere. Clearly, the participative approach would be more effective with today's work force.

What characterizes participative management? First of all, it involves delegating to employees both the task *and* the authority for a variety of job activities. It is giving individual employees not only the opportunity to find out the facts about a problem but the authority, within limits, to determine and implement the solution to the problem. It is giving employees the discretion and autonomy to run their own shows, to be intrapreneurs within the company. Participative management of this nature is not a loss of control, as feared by some managers, but rather the fullest, and smartest, use of the company's human resources.

Participative management in the human resources period will involve a greater sharing of job responsibilities, with a narrowing of the differences between supervisory and nonsupervisory jobs. Supervisors will "take over" from their assistants tasks such as preparing memos, and assistants, in turn, will pick up activities such as project or budget work formerly carried out by supervisors. This sharing of responsibilities will not happen by itself but must be actively managed by supervisors.

Participative management will involve decision making at the lowest possible level and employee self-management wherever possible. The case of the Dana truck axle plant described in Chapter Five showed the extreme version of self-management. Here there were no levels of supervision, but only employee self-management. Participative management will also involve decentralizing control as well as staff—locating more jobs at the local level rather than corporate headquarters. Rockwell International, one of the top twenty companies in the Survey of Organizations, has a management philosophy that "encourages individual initiative at its business units and supports that initiative with financial and technical resources." Such an attitude is very effective for the human resources period.

How common is participative management? Is it related to a company's financial success? Of the top twenty companies in our survey, *every one* described its management style as "very participative." Altogether, 70 percent of the highly progressive, highly profitable companies described their style as very participative. Of the less progressive companies, with poorer financial results, only 4 percent saw their management style as very participative. Clearly, a very participative management style leads to better sales growth, higher profit margins, and other key financial benefits.

Fostering Creativity

Another key management skill for the future is fostering creativity in *all* employees. In the industrial period, creative efforts were the province of a select few. Managers, engineers, and scientists were essentially the only employees responsible for creating or modifying products and services. Creativity on the part of the typical employee was actually discouraged in many companies in the early part of the twentieth century. The role of the typical employee was to implement what was developed by someone else. Many managers still see it as their responsibility to create and innovate, rather than tap their staff's ideas as well.

The need to have everyone involved in creative efforts is being fueled by several factors. The first of these is the fact that we have recently seen the introduction of new industries and new technology. Getting the most out of these new industries and technology requires the creative efforts of a large number of people, not just a select group of managers and specialists. Companies that reserve creative improvements for only a select few will not be getting the most out of their human resources. The success of their products and services will suffer as a result.

In addition, the pace of change in the workplace seems quicker than ever before. Much of this is a result of the magnitude of the human resources revolution, a workplace change greater than any other in the past few hundred years. But how do you introduce this change effectively? How do you make the countless decisions on how to best implement this change? If the onus is on one person, the manager, to plan and implement all of the change, results may suffer. With the entire staff helping to plan, implement, and manage this rapid change, results will likely be better.

A last factor fueling the need for creative efforts by all is the development of new jobs. As we reviewed earlier, the trend here is for growth in white-collar and service jobs that are more generalist in nature. These jobs *require* creative efforts for employees to carry out their responsibilities. And the complexity of jobs and number of immediate subordinates will make it impossible for any manager to solve all problems and be the expert at all jobs. More effective managers will tap the creative ideas of their staffs.

How should managers tap the creative efforts of all? First, the company culture should emphasize that creativity is a part of everyone's job, not just the jobs of a select few. This can be stated in job descriptions. Companies such as Tandem Computers have been very successful in getting across this idea. Second, managers must manage with this idea in mind and be held accountable for results. They must take action with their respective staffs to ensure that creativity is tapped and that everyone has a role in change. Management training courses can be used to help build skills in tapping creativity. Managers' skill at using employees' creative ideas should be reflected in their performance appraisals, building in accountability for managing this way.

Day-to-day management of creativity should reflect an open encouragement of new ideas. Managers should be seeking from their staffs newer, better, and different ways of doing things. The manager's role here becomes that of a catalyst or "cheerleader" for encouraging improvements and creative change in the workplace. And, of course, at least some of the ideas employees come up with must be implemented, or the creative effort will be seen only as a waste of time.

One of the things an industrial-period manager might find most difficult to do is asking the staff for help in solving a problem. Such "old school" managers might feel that they were hired to carry out such activities themselves and see it as humbling to ask their staffs for help. But a manager of the human resources period will have no qualms about asking others for their ideas in solving a problem. This will be seen as a smart and effective use of the entire staff, leading to a better solution than the manager could generate alone.

Are managers of leading companies managing creativity as we suggest here? The Survey of Organizations showed that, of the companies high in human resources progressiveness and highly successful, 62 percent had managers who strongly encouraged employee creativity. Of the companies low in human resources progressiveness and less successful, only 10 percent had managers who strongly encouraged employee creativity. Very clearly, fostering creativity is related to financial success. Those companies that involve employees in creative efforts enjoy better financial results than those that do not.

Enhancing Communications

Management communications skills have always played an important role in the workplace. That importance will increase with changes in the work environment, such as the demographics of the new work force. Employees are now more likely to be members of minority groups, female, or recent immigrants. As a result, supervisors will have to develop a better understanding of employee needs, be effective listeners, and communicate clearly to those who may not speak English fluently.

Other changes affecting communications are the decentralizing of the workplace and the movement of work into the home. As a result of these trends, supervisors may not be at the same physical location as their employees. Communications will be less frequent and more likely to take place through writing or over the phone than in face-to-face meetings. This creates a greater need for effective communications.

A last change worth noting is the nature of the new jobs. The types of positions being created require interaction with clients and customers, though not necessarily in face-to-face meetings. Employee communications skills will need to be sharp, and supervisors will need to provide training and coaching. If the supervisor is not a good role model for communications skills, employees will not learn effectively. This is still another reason for excellent management communications skills.

The first element of effective management communications is mastering the mechanics. Speaking clearly and concisely is a prerequisite for any type of communication. Speaking skills are enhanced by the effective use of gestures and body language. Perhaps the most important management communications skill is listening. In the past, managers spent more time talking than listening, but listening will become increasingly important in the service environment of the future. All managers should receive training in basic communications skills.

The *content* of what managers need to communicate starts with the company culture—the big picture of the company's products, services, uniqueness, and values. Employees in distant locations will particularly need this information. The communication on culture should include a strong message that employees are the most important asset. Effective managers of the human resources period will genuinely believe this and communicate it often.

Managers will also need to strongly communicate the mission and goals of their areas of responsibility. Each employee should be aware of both departmental and personal goals for the coming year. This sense of direction is necessary for employees to focus their efforts. The Survey of Organizations found that 80 percent of the companies progressive in human resources have clear goals for their employees. Only 26 percent of the less progressive companies do. Since human resources progressiveness is related to company financial success, there is good reason for communicating and utilizing goals. Those companies that did so attained better financial results than those who did not.

A last element of effective management communications is the open-door policy. Managers' use of the open-door policy at all times and their practice of trust and openness in their communications will set a tone and climate for candid exchanges between supervisors and employees and make for better working relationships. To supplement this, open-forum meetings can give employees the opportunity to raise issues of concern to them. Skip-level meetings, between an employee and the boss of the employee's boss, are still another means of implementing open-door policies. The open door fits in well with the human resources period.

Technology can enhance management communications, particularly across locations that are far apart. Such technology might include teleconferencing, electronic mail, and facsimile machines. Are companies today making use of the latest communications technology? The Survey of Organizations found that 72 percent of the highly progressive, highly successful companies made use of the latest communications technology. Only 28 percent of the less progressive, less successful companies used it. It would appear that investing in this technology pays off in the form of better financial results, since the more progressive companies were more financially successful.

Staff Selection and Development

The area of staff selection and development was less important during the industrial period, when jobs were simple and easy to learn, making selection and development easy to carry out. The jobs of today are more complex, making selection decisions more difficult and making training a lengthier, more complex process. Further, the employees of today, as we mentioned earlier, want a career rather than just a job. Management skill at selecting and developing a staff will have a major impact on the company's success.

What types of management skills are needed in selection and development? The skills and traits that managers should look for in new employees and the progressive selection practices that should be used in hiring were discussed in Chapter Eight. In hiring managers, interpersonal skills should take precedence over technical job knowledge. Though the reverse may have been practiced in the industrial period, all the evidence that we have presented shows the importance of the human side of management. Selecting managers with strong interpersonal skills will help ensure that the benefits described in this book are actually attained.

Managers will also need to show skill in managing alternative employment arrangements. Progressive managers have come to recognize that the human resources required for an assignment need not come from full-time staff. Part-time employees, contractors, and retirees are all viable options for filling human resources needs. Managers of the human resources period will not only recognize these possibilities but actively set up such alternative employment options for their areas of responsibility.

In the area of development, managers must be skilled in the role of coach and counselor. Managers of the human resources period will see employee development not as a task that takes up time but as a benefit that fulfills employee needs and results in a more productive work force. Providing feedback in performance appraisals will not be seen as a requirement to be halfheartedly fulfilled but as a chance to develop employee skills to new levels. In the role of coach and counselor for performance improvement, the manager's approach should not be "You must improve or else," but rather should be, "We are in this together, so let's figure out a way to make it better." That type of management skill and style will lead to success in the coming years.

Managers will also need skills in providing career guidance to employees. This function will be seen as an opportunity to ideally match employee interests and abilities with various jobs in the company. That permits the company to best utilize its human resources. Candid feedback and discussion of career options will be part of the manager's role in career guidance. The manager of the human resources period will help employees attain needed skills and knowledge to reach their career goals. This could be provided through in-house or outside courses, professional associations, mentoring, or direct training from the manager. When employees are ready for another position, their movement to another department will be seen not as a loss but rather as a gain for the company.

Action Steps for the Human Resources or Line Manager

It is important that managers at your company manage in a way that is compatible with the human resources period. To ensure that this happens, the following action steps may be taken:

1. Evaluate your current management style and the skill levels of individuals. Are you managing in a tight, controlling manner, or providing "general" supervision as defined in this chapter? Is the management style participative? Do managers foster creativity? Are they skilled at communications and staff selection and development? These are the key areas for success during the human resources period.

2. Where the management style needs changing, training and development should be provided. This is best done through in-house courses, which should have a practical, skill-building approach. Having the senior managers attend and support such training is essential for success. Outside seminars and individual development programs can also be used to build skills. Chapter Nine provided details on the establishment of such training programs.

3. After the training is completed, ongoing reinforcement of the suggested management skills and style is needed. This can be done, for example, by having the CEO demonstrate support verbally and in writing. The company culture should also address the key elements of management covered in this chapter. This will continually remind managers of the suggested practices. Periodic company publications could also reinforce the desired management practices. Stories might cite particularly effective examples of management behavior or expand on the key ideas. And the performance appraisal process should reflect the key elements of management. Managers should be evaluated, for example, on how well they practice participative management and how well they foster creativity. With such ongoing reinforcement, there is a greater likelihood that managers will continually be reminded of and reinforced for practicing effective management.

Summary

A new way of managing is essential if the benefits of the human resources period are to be attained. The autocratic style that has persisted to the present time will negate nearly all of the potential benefits from new technology, new jobs, a new work force, and a new workplace. The human resources period offers tremendous potential for both companies and individual employees, but only if the management style is in concert with the workplace. That new management style will eliminate tight controls, unnecessary workplace rules, and decisions made by only a few. In its place, there will be more general supervision, providing guidance and direction to staff, broadening employee job roles, building teamwork, and doing what is right for the individual rather than relying on policies.

Participative management is the key element for managers in the human resources period. Participative managers will delegate both the task *and* the authority to subordinates. Decisions will be delegated to the lowest possible level. There will be more sharing of responsibilities as the difference between jobs becomes narrower. Managers of the human resources period will also foster creativity in their employees. They will see that creative efforts are a part of everyone's job and use the ideas and suggestions that others come up with.

Enhanced communications skills will be particularly critical in the coming years. Managers will have to be adept at the mechanics of communicating, particularly listening skills. They will need to strongly communicate a vision for the future, where the company is going, its mission and goals. In addition, managers will practice the open-door policy and trust and candidness in dealing with employees.

Finally, managers need to use the latest hiring techniques and select for a broad array of skills. Managers will also take on a key role in facilitating career development through providing candid feedback, making training available, and supporting the movement of employees into their preferred areas.

In this book, we have discussed a number of dramatic changes that have occurred in the workplace. These changes include new technology, new organizational structures, new workplaces, and a different work force, with a resulting need for a change in management style. The human resources period offers a unique opportunity for companies, an opportunity not encountered in the past few hundred years, since the start of the industrial revolution. Those who can pull back, evaluate their practices, and adjust where necessary will enjoy the benefits of being in tune with the new workplace.

The Survey of Organizations, which was cited often, offered compelling evidence that human resources progressiveness is related to company financial results. Companies that were progressive enjoyed better sales growth, better profit margins, and better earnings per share than their less progressive counterparts. The suggestions offered in this book, such as having a strongly people-oriented culture, decentralizing the work environment, creating meaningful jobs, and using participative management, were offered not just because they make sense but because they also lead to better financial results.

The many examples and case studies drawn from leading companies should make it easier for human resources and line managers to implement the suggested practices at their companies. The choice as to how to proceed is now up to each employee and each company. Many have taken the path of progressive human resources practices and enjoyed the results. Others have clung to the old way of doing things, hoping that the ''market will get better'' or that the ''union will come to its senses.'' Those who clearly understand where the workplace is going will choose progressive human resources practices. Be one of them and make it happen at your company.

Appendix:
Notes on the
Survey of Organizations

Presented below is the Survey of Organizations questionnaire as it was sent to the target companies. Following the questionnaire, we present details on the construction of the questionnaire, pilot testing, the survey population, and the results of our analysis of responses to the questionnaire.

Table 6. The Survey of Organizations.

Note: Please be candid in your responses and be certain to answer each question. Your answers to some questions might depend upon which division, subsidiary, or employee job group you consider within your company. When answering such questions, think of your company on the whole, and respond as you would for the most typical situation in your company. Thanks for your cooperation.

Circle the appropriate number after each question by using the following scale:

1. Strongly disagree
2. Disagree
3. Uncertain
4. Agree
5. Strongly agree

1. The average manager in my company understands the company's overall goals and priorities.   1 2 3 4 5
2. The average employee (nonmanager) in my company understands the company's overall goals and priorities.   1 2 3 4 5

Table 6. The Survey of Organizations, Cont'd.

---

3. Company financial results are shared with all employees in the company.   1 2 3 4 5

4. My company's operating philosophy and "culture" are understood by the majority of employees.   1 2 3 4 5

5. The company operating philosophy and "culture" place a high emphasis on people.   1 2 3 4 5

6. Our managers practice the open-door philosophy to a high degree.   1 2 3 4 5

7. My company makes use of recent communications techniques (for example, teleconferencing, electronic mail, videotapes of executive presentations).   1 2 3 4 5

8. Our company's overall management style could be described as very participative.   1 2 3 4 5

9. The average employee in my company is frequently sought out for his or her ideas.   1 2 3 4 5

10. My company delegates responsibility to the lowest possible level.   1 2 3 4 5

11. In the past couple of years, there has been a trend in my company to have more generalist as opposed to specialist jobs.   1 2 3 4 5

12. The typical job in my company is more generalist than specialist.   1 2 3 4 5

13. Managers in my company strongly encourage individual creativity on the job.   1 2 3 4 5

14. Our company is strongly oriented toward our customers.   1 2 3 4 5

15. My company's management consistently emphasizes excellence in the workplace and high-quality results.   1 2 3 4 5

16. My company works hard toward building job satisfaction (for example, uses job attitude surveys, has open discussions of problems).   1 2 3 4 5

17. Employees in my company are encouraged to own a part of the company through stock purchase or other means. (Leave blank if private or nonprofit company.)   1 2 3 4 5

If applicable, what percentage of your employees own stock in the company?
1. 0–20%
2. 21–40%
3. 41–60%
4. 61–80%
5. 81–100%

Table 6. The Survey of Organizations, Cont'd.

---

18. We handle employee relations matters on an individual basis rather than "go by the book." 1 2 3 4 5
19. The majority of my company's operating facilities are unionized. 1. Yes 2. No
20. We try to hire the highest-quality job candidates, regardless of the cost. 1 2 3 4 5
21. Outstanding job candidates at my company typically would *not* be screened out if they earned above the maximum for the job. 1 2 3 4 5
22. Management succession plans are in place for the majority of management jobs at my company. 1 2 3 4 5
23. Human resources planning is well integrated with strategic planning at our company. 1 2 3 4 5
24. A job candidate's creativity is an important part of the selection process at our company. 1 2 3 4 5
25. In addition to the job interview, we typically use other types of selection procedures (for example, tests, assessment center, job simulations). 1 2 3 4 5
26. How much time is devoted to formal orientation programs for new hires (exclude technical training, management development programs, and on-the-job coaching)?
    1. No programs
    2. 0–7 hours
    3. 1–2 days
    4. 3–5 days
    5. 6 days +
27. How many *days* of in-house management development programs would a typical first-line manager have access to (exclude technical training)?
    1. None
    2. 1–5
    3. 6–10
    4. 11–15
    5. 16 or more
28. My company does a good job at providing technical training for employees. 1 2 3 4 5
29. If someone at my company is switching career areas (for example, secretary to programmer/analyst), we provide technical training to assist the career move. 1 2 3 4 5
30. What percentage of tuition is reimbursed for approved college courses at your company (assume course is passed)?
    1. None
    2. 1–50%
    3. 51–75%
    4. 76–90%
    5. 91–100%
31. A typical professional employee at our company attends one or more out-of-town conferences or seminars during the course of a year. 1 2 3 4 5
32. My company has some type of career planning program available for employees. 1 2 3 4 5

Table 6. The Survey of Organizations, Cont'd.

33. A typical employee at our company would understand career paths from his or her job and what it takes to attain other jobs of interest.   1 2 3 4 5

34. The majority of employees at my company have performance goals for their jobs.   1 2 3 4 5

35. Written performance appraisals are given to employees at least once a year.   1 2 3 4 5

36. We are currently doing a fine job at appraising employee job performance.   1 2 3 4 5

37. Salary increases are definitely based on job performance at our company.   1 2 3 4 5

38. We allow employees to choose the unique mix of benefits that they want (some version of a cafeteria plan).   1 2 3 4 5

39. Special achievements of a short-term nature would be rewarded by my company through gifts, stock, a night on the town, or other means.   1 2 3 4 5

40. The majority of our facilities use some form of flextime.   1 2 3 4 5

41. Some of our employees currently work out of their homes.
   1. No
   2. Yes

         If yes, estimated percentage.
   1. 0–2%
   2. 3–5%
   3. 6–9%
   4. 10–19%
   5. 20% or more

42. Our company has seen an increase in the number of part-time employees in the past couple of years (exclude temporary agencies).   1 2 3 4 5

43. We have cases where two or more employees share the same job, each working part time.   1 2 3 4 5

44. At most of our facilities, there is *no* set time for employees to take a lunch break.   1 2 3 4 5

45. My company takes advantage of the latest technology in the workplace (for example, word processors, robots, telecommunications devices).   1 2 3 4 5

46. My company's operations are concentrating more and more in the South and West portions of the United States.   1 2 3 4 5

47. If an employee requested a transfer to another location, we would provide relocation assistance.   1 2 3 4 5

48. My company has a flat management hierarchy.   1 2 3 4 5

49. Our company is very decentralized in its operations.   1 2 3 4 5

50. Our plans for the future call for small facilities rather than large, concentrated facilities.   1 2 3 4 5

Table 6. The Survey of Organizations, Cont'd.

---

51. The majority of jobs in our company are white
    collar or service.   1 2 3 4 5
52. Select the best industry code for your company:
    _____   1. Mining, oil, and refining.
    _____   2. Food and related products.
    _____   3. Textiles and apparel.
    _____   4. Furniture, paper, and wood products.
    _____   5. Publishing and printing.
    _____   6. Chemical, pharmaceuticals, and allied products.
    _____   7. Rubber, plastic, and glass products.
    _____   8. Metal manufacturing and metal products.
    _____   9. Machinery (except electrical).
    _____   10. Electrical/electronic products (including computers
               and office equipment).
    _____   11. Ships, railroads, and transportation equipment.
    _____   12. Measuring, scientific, and photographic equipment.
    _____   13. Communications and utilities.
    _____   14. Wholesale and retail trade.
    _____   15. Finance and insurance.
    _____   16. Service companies.
53. Last year's annual sales:
    1. $0–249 million.
    2. $250–499 million.
    3. $500–999 million.
    4. $1–5 billion.
    5. $6 billion or more.

Conducting the Survey

Questionnaire Construction. A total of seventy-three items were originally developed to assess human resources progressiveness. These items covered a wide variety of areas revolving around emerging trends in the workplace. Nearly all items were based on a five-point Likert scale, with higher values indicating greater human resources progressiveness.

Sample Testing. A pilot test was done with the questionnaire before it was sent out to the larger population. The purpose of the pilot test was to evaluate the items and delete or modify them as needed. A total of fifty-two managers in twenty-one different companies served as the pilot test group. Since only the items were being tested, there were no problems with having multiple raters from the same company. None of these pilot testing companies was used in the larger population survey.

Pilot Results. Responses on the seventy-three items were put through factor analysis procedures. This statistical technique was used to identify the main dimensions to the questionnaire and help eliminate unnecessary items. Results from the factor analysis suggested that the number of items could be reduced to fifty-one. The deleted items did not contribute to interpreting the results, largely because other items measured similar attributes. The final questionnaire used with the larger population consisted of fifty-one items relating to human resources practices, plus two items establishing industry type and sales volume. The major dimensions of the questionnaire, as identified through the factor analysis, were as follows:

1. A "general factor"—many items loaded on a single dimension that was interpreted as human resources progressiveness
2. Degree of emphasis on people in the company culture
3. Degree of participative management
4. Communications progressiveness
5. Extent of career development and training
6. Degree of recognition and reward for good performance
7. Use of flextime, work at home, and part-time employment
8. Degree of decentralization and flat management hierarchy

Survey Population. The *Forbes* 500 list ("The 500 Annual Directory," 1984) served as the starting point for selecting companies for the Survey of Organizations. Since this list does not include banks and other financial services companies, 42 large organizations of this type were added to the survey population. Some of the smaller companies on the *Forbes* 500 list were deleted so that the final group to be surveyed was exactly 500, including banks.

Directions emphasized that the questionnaire was a survey of human resources practices and that responses would be kept confidential. To avoid bias, no mention was made that item responses would be correlated with financial success. The financial results on each company were collected independently through publicly released financial statements.

There were no follow-up efforts to increase the response rate beyond the 159 who returned questionnaires from the initial mailing. Six companies were eliminated from the study because of incomplete financial information or recent mergers or acquisitions. Three companies were eliminated because of incomplete questionnaires. The final group retained for the study was 150 companies. Many of the 150 companies in the study were contacted for phone interviews. The purpose of the interviews was to confirm the responses and ask the firms to cite specific examples of their practices. A very small percentage (.2 percent) of item responses were changed on the basis of the phone conversations.

Scoring of Questionnaires. It was decided to score each questionnaire by merely summing the scores of the human resources progressiveness items. The reasons for doing this were that:

1. The factor analysis identified a general factor, labeled "human resources progressiveness," that was made up of many individual questionnaire items
2. It was hypothesized that overall human resources progressiveness, as a general company trend, would be related to financial results
3. Overall human resources progressiveness was an easy concept to understand

Overall Results

Table 7 presents the means and standard deviations on financial results for all 150 companies. The last two columns present the same figures for the pooled sample, which included only the companies high or low in human resources progressiveness. The pooling of standard deviations followed the procedure suggested in McNemar (1962).

T tests were used to determine whether there were sig-

Table 7. The Survey of Organizations:
Means and Standard Deviations.

Financial Result	Entire Sample (N = 150)		Pooled Sample[a] (N = 100)	
	Mean	Standard Deviation	Mean	Standard Deviation
Annualized sales growth, five-year trend	14.92	19.54	14.12	14.77
Annualized profit growth, five-year trend	5.85	20.07	6.74	21.07
Latest annual profit margin	4.16	3.30	4.31	3.45
Annualized equity growth, five-year trend	11.67	13.48	12.99	14.81
Annualized growth in earnings per share, five-year trend	1.78	19.68	1.18	17.14
Latest price-earnings ratio	13.38	13.97	14.44	16.12
Annualized dividend growth, five-year trend	10.55	13.17	11.34	14.84

[a]The pooled sample, consisting of those high in human resources progressiveness plus those low in human resources progressiveness, was used in calculating the biserial correlations.

nificant group differences on each of the financial results. In each case, a t test was run to contrast the means of the highly progressive and less progressive groups. The t test procedure was that used in Hays (1973). The f test of differences in group standard deviations followed the procedure in Downie and Heath (1965).

All t tests reached at least the .05 level of significance except two, dividend growth (significant at the .10 level) and the price-earnings ratio, which was not statistically significant. These findings indicated very strong support for the notion that human resources progressiveness is related to company financial results.

Biserial correlations (see Downie and Heath, 1965) were run between the human resources progressiveness score and each financial result. The findings are presented in Table 8. As can be seen, five of the seven correlations reached conventional significance levels, with one additional result significant at the .10 level. Once again, support was strong for a relationship between human resources progressiveness and company financial results.

Table 8. The Survey of Organizations: Correlations.

Financial Result	Correlation with Human Resources Progressiveness[a]	Significance Level
Annualized sales growth, five-year trend	.29	.025
Annualized profit growth, five-year trend	.24	.05
Latest annual profit margin	.37	.005
Annualized equity growth, five-year trend	.31	.01
Annualized growth in earnings per share, five-year trend	.37	.005
Latest price-earnings ratio	.05	n.s.
Annualized dividend growth, five-year trend	.18	.10

[a]Correlations are biserial correlations (N = 100). The standard error for each correlation was .125.

References

AFL-CIO Committee on the Evolution of Work. *Report to the Executive Council.* Washington, D.C.: AFL-CIO, 1983.

American Society for Personnel Administration. "Membership Survey." *Resource,* June 1986, p. 1.

Balkin, D., and Gomez-Mejia, L. "Compensation Practices in High-Technology Industries." *Personnel Administrator,* June 1985, pp. 111–123.

Bronowski, J. *The Ascent of Man.* Boston: Little, Brown, 1973.

Choate, P. Untitled article. In *Work in the 21st Century.* Arlington, Va.: American Society for Personnel Administration, 1983.

Commerce Clearing House. "1987 ASPA/CCH Survey." *Human Resources Management,* June 26, 1987, pp. 1–15.

Downie, N., and Heath, R. *Basic Statistical Methods.* New York: Harper & Row, 1965.

Electronic Services Unlimited. *Telecommuting: Its Potential Effects on Profits and Productivity.* New York: Electronic Services Unlimited, 1986.

Feingold, N. Untitled article. In *Work in the 21st Century.* Arlington, Va.: American Society for Personnel Administration, 1983.

"The 500 Annual Directory." *Forbes,* Apr. 30, 1984.

Gordon, G., and Kelly, M. *Telecommuting.* Englewood Cliffs, N.J.: Prentice-Hall, 1986.

Hays, W. *Statistics for the Social Sciences.* (2nd ed.) New York: Holt, Rinehart & Winston, 1973.

Heisler, W., and Houch, J. *A Matter of Dignity.* South Bend, Ind.: University of Notre Dame Press, 1977.

Holland, J. *Making Vocational Choices: A Theory of Careers.* Englewood Cliffs, N.J.: Prentice-Hall, 1973.

"Industry Report 1986." *Training,* Oct. 1986, pp. 26–83.

Judkins, P., West, D., and Drew, J. *Networking in Organizations: The Rank Xerox Experiment.* Aldershot, England: Gower, 1985.

Kearns, R. "Steel Industry Takes Turn for Worse." *Chicago Tribune,* Nov. 11, 1984, Business Section, p. 1.

Klaus, G. Untitled article. In *Work in the 21st Century.* Arlington, Va.: American Society for Personnel Administration, 1983.

Lawler, E. *Pay and Organizational Effectiveness.* New York: McGraw-Hill, 1971.

"Living Alone: Who, Why, the Pleasures, the Pitfalls." *Chicago Tribune,* June 7, 1987, pp. 1–6.

McNemar, Q. *Psychological Statistics.* (3rd ed.) New York: Wiley, 1962.

Maslow, A. H. *Motivation and Personality.* New York: Harper & Row, 1954.

National Research Council's Manufacturers Studies Board. "Toward a New Era in U.S. Manufacturing." In W. Neikirk, "Spree May Be Ending for Overseas Moves." *Chicago Tribune,* July 5, 1987, p. 14.

"1984 Scoreboard Special Issue." *Business Week,* Mar. 21, 1984 (entire issue).

Peters, T., and Waterman, R. *In Search of Excellence: Lessons from America's Best Run Companies.* New York: Harper & Row, 1982.

Rogers, D. *The Work Ethic in Industrial America, 1850–1920.* Chicago: University of Chicago Press, 1974.

Rosow, J., and Zager, R. *Productivity Through Work Innovations.* New York: Pergamon Press, 1982.

Rothberg, D., and Ensor, B. *Part-Time Professional.* Washington, D.C.: Acropolis, 1985.

"Statement of Corporate Purpose." In-house document, Prime Computer, Natick, Mass., n.d.

Toffler, A. *The Third Wave.* New York: Morrow, 1980.

U.S. Bureau of Labor Statistics. "White Males Lose Work Force Majority Status, BLS Says." *Resource,* Sept. 1984, p. 9.

U.S. Department of Commerce. *Historical Statistics of the United States, Part I and Part II.* Washington, D.C.: U.S. Department of Commerce, 1975.

The U.S. Industrial Outlook, 1985: Prospects for over 350 Manufacturing and Services Industries. (26th ed.) Washington, D.C.: U.S. Government Printing Office, 1985.

U.S. Office of Technology Assessment. *Computerized Manufacturing Automation—Employment, Education and the Work Place.* Washington, D.C.: U.S. Office of Technology Assessment, 1984.

Wattenberg, B. *The Birth Dearth.* New York: Pharos, 1987.

Watts, G. Untitled article. In *Work in the 21st Century.* Arlington, Va.: American Society for Personnel Administration, 1983.

"Working by Wire." *Forbes,* Feb. 11, 1985, pp. 14–15.

World Future Society. *Annual Report.* Bethesda, Md.: World Future Society, 1984.

Yankelovich, D., and Immewahr, J. *Putting the Work Ethic to Work.* New York: Public Agenda Foundation, 1983.

Zemke, R. "Training in the 90s." *Training,* Jan. 1987, pp. 40–53.

Index